The

Offshore Race Crew's
Manual

The

Offshore Race Crew's
Manual

By
Stuart Quarrie

WATERLINE

By the same author

Navigation, Strategy and Tactics
published by Guardian Newspapers Ltd.

Quarrie on Racing
published by Waterline Books

The photographs in this book are courtesy of *Yachting World* magazine with the
exception of the following:
Pages 148 and 149 courtesy of Henri Lloyd Ltd.

The illustrations are by Peter Coles.

Published by Waterline Books
an imprint of Airlife Publishing Ltd,
101 Longden Rd, Shrewsbury, England

ISBN 1 85310 510 4

A Sheerstrake production.

A CIP catalogue record of this book
is available from the British Library

Printed in Singapore by Kyodo Printing Co. (S'pore) Pte Ltd.

Contents

Chapter 3
Sail Trim

Chapter 4
Setting Up For An Offshore Race

Après Sail.

Introduction

This is a book written by someone who genuinely enjoys offshore racing and who has sailed on hundreds of different yachts at all levels and in most types of race. It is intended to help crew members of either sex, and at any age and level of experience. A large part of the book concentrates on actual crew work and manoeuvres but there are also sections on watch systems, victuals, heavy weather, sail trim and setting-up the yacht for racing.

Offshore crewing, whether during a race or while cruising is great fun, but can be physically demanding and takes a high degree of commitment from participants. Racing in particular requires the entire the crew to have a common aim and for every member to put maximum effort into winning. Sailing is sometimes lovely, spinnaker reaching in a flat sea and sunny conditions, or it can be really bloody, as when going to windward in freezing conditions and half a gale – but it is always worth the experience. The sense of personal achievement after finishing a race or passage and knowing that you have contributed as much as possible to the running of the yacht is a great feeling. Most of the preparation and manoeuvres are simple in themselves but it is important to understand what is required and then how to execute each to a high level of perfection. Trying to re-invent the wheel each time a new situation is encountered is not very efficient and does not win races. One way to learn is to listen to others who just might have been in the same situation before.

I enjoy coaching at all levels and this book is merely an extension of coaching afloat. My ideas evolved as my experience grows; sailing with different people allows me to see differing ways of doing the same things. There is rarely a 'right' way to do something, it is merely that some methods seem to be generally more efficient than others. I do not pretend that this is a bible for everyone to follow. I shall be happy enough if every reader either learns something new or even just uses my experience to rethink how he or she goes about racing.

Stuart Quarrie 1994
Lymington
England

Chapter 1
Crew Work By Manoeuvre

In this section we shall look at the detail of each manoeuvre; at who does what and in what order, the priorities and where potential problems can occur. Whatever type of manoeuvre you are about to attempt, the most important thing is to be organised. The whole crew needs to know what is required of them and ideally you will have practised the manoeuvre in a non-racing environment before attempting it in a stressful situation. Few manoeuvres are really complicated but most can be ruined if the basics are not carried out efficiently. If all crew members understand what is going to happen and how their own job can affect others, then life will be easier for everyone.

Tacking in Moderate Airs

This is a manoeuvre which happens so frequently that it is often ignored in any practise sessions, being thought of as too basic to need comment. One should remember that because it is executed so often during a race, small gains on each tack can have a significant effect on the overall performance. Also, in many cases you will be tacking at critical times, often with another yacht close by and when any mistake, however small, can leave you in dirty air and force you to tack away again.

The principle of a good tack is simple enough. The yacht should be sailing at maximum speed until you actually commence the tack. The tack itself should happen with the minimum loss of speed and you should then get back up to your optimum speed as quickly as possible. In practice of course it is not quite as easy as it sounds.

When 'Ready About' is called, those crew members who must move from the side-deck should do so in an agreed order. Those who are not needed to prepare for the tack should stay

sitting-out and if possible should hike out even harder than before to keep the yacht on her feet. In practice this means that the person letting off the old sheet must move into the cockpit, ensure the new sheet is on the winch with a handle in and that the old sheet is uncleated, winch handle out and ready to let fly. If you have runners, these must also be set up by another crewman. At the same time, the mainsheet trimmer needs to prepare by ensuring the traveller controls are set for tacking and take the sheet in hand.

Each yacht has a different system of calling to advise when the crew is ready to tack. This can either be done on a positive call from each relevant crewman that he is ready or on a negative response if there is a problem. Although both systems have their pros and cons, I tend to favour the latter negative response system, especially for crews who sail together on a regular basis.

Photo 1.1 On the call 'Ready About', one crew member leaves the rail to prepare the working winch for the tack by removing the handle and uncleating the sheet. The rest stay on the rail.

Once the crew are ready, it is up to the helmsman to time the tack itself. He should ensure that the speed is good and if possible find a relatively flat patch of water to tack into, or if that is not feasible at least to ensure that he does not tack straight into the face of an oncoming wave.

Immediately before putting the helm over, he should call 'tacking' or 'lee-ho' or something similar to warn the whole crew that the manoeuvre is starting. At this point many things happen at once.

1. The tailer for the new sheet comes off the rail and gets ready to pull the sail around. On most yachts it will be best if he takes the tail across the cockpit to the new high side as the sail comes around so that he ends up tailing the final amount from the new windward side.

2. The new runner is pulled as tight as it can be against the mainsail and as the yacht turns is kept tight, then once the main has crossed the centreline the old runner is released and tension wound on to the new one.

Photo 1.2 Tensioning and releasing the runners is a vital job on a fractional rig during a tack.

3. The trimmer lets go the old sheet as pressure comes off and just a fraction of a second before the sail goes aback. If he leaves it too late the spreaders might go through the sail or if he lets go too early, then the sail will beat itself to death on the mast and rig and will inevitably get snagged half way round. He should leave a half or quarter turn of the old sheet around the winch so that any kinks are stripped out of the rope before going to the new side to wind in the new sheet. On really large yachts, it may be necessary to have separate grinders, either at the winch or on a grinding pedestal, but on moderate sized yachts, up to about twelve metres (40 ft), the trimmer should be able to manage alone.

4. The mainsail trimmer should pull the traveller to windward as the yacht starts to turn, thus keeping the sail full for as long as possible. Once the sail flaps he should ease a few centimetres of sheet (possibly by dumping the fine-tune?), move to the new side and pull the traveller up. He then gradually drops it back down the track as the yacht bears away. This gets the sail full as early through the tack as possible while allowing speed to build fast out of the tack. As speed builds, the traveller can be pulled back up to its normal position and the sheet tensioned again.

5. The bowman should move to the mast, help the sail around it if needed and then be ready to skirt the foot over the guard-rail if it snags.

6. One of the middle crew should be responsible for ensuring the old sheet does not snag as it is let fly and for clearing it if it does get caught on anything.

7. All other crew should wait until the boat starts to come upright and then rapidly dive across to sit-out on the new side.

Photo 1.3 The bowman 'skirts' the foot of the genoa when it gets caught on the guard-rail

The yacht can be turned as far as head to wind quite fast but once the genoa is through to the new side the turn needs to be slowed down. Remember that speed is bound to drop during a tack so sails will need to be slightly looser as you come out of the tack to take account of the decreased apparent wind. The other major point to bear in mind is that you must get up close to target speed before coming really hard on the wind after the tack. Pinching into the wind will mean the keel is not working efficiently at the low speed and the whole rig will not be operating as well as it might, so stay a degree or two off the normal angles until speed has returned. If tacking with a large genoa at or near the top of its wind range, it may be necessary to pinch slightly just for a few moments to give the grinder the chance to get it fully wound in, but then bear off a few degrees to build speed as rapidly as possible.

Photo 1.4 Having completed the tack, the crew should all get back to the weather rail and hike-out hard to get the boat back to optimum speed.

Tacking – Light Airs

Here the problems are somewhat different. The crew is likely to be sitting to leeward and the most important consideration is to not lose any more boat speed than is absolutely necessary. Pointing after the tack will be impossible until the speed has built up again and from the crews' point of view, it is essential to move gently and to get the yacht heeling to leeward again. On small to medium sized yachts it may be possible to 'roll tack' as in a dinghy, keeping the yacht heeled to leeward until she goes head to wind and then rapidly moving crew weight to the other side, possibly having the crew standing and leaning hard out against the guard-rails.

Timing the tack is even more crucial than in moderate airs. Whenever possible the manoeuvre should be carried out in a gust or at the very least a slight breeze, but never in a lull. Good speed going into the tack will help to ensure a quick tack; it may be necessary for the trimmers to ease sheets slightly before the tack and for the helmsman to sail a few degrees low in order to encourage good boat speed. Runners are unlikely to be critical, except letting off the old runner to prevent it interfering with the mainsail and on most yachts one or at the most two crew should be able to work the sheets in the cockpit.

On 'Ready About' being called, the trimmer (who will be at his sheet anyway) prepares both winches for tacking and prepares to let off the old sheet. As described above, he and the mainsheet trimmer probably also crack sheets a touch and the helmsman sails the boat a bit 'fat' to increase speed.

Once you roll into the tack, all the crew except the trimmers and bowman get to the new leeward side. If some were sitting to windward before the tack, they must stay down to leeward until well after the tack has been completed. The old sheet is let off smoothly as the sail starts to go aback and the bowman helps it around the rig. The new sheet is pulled in smoothly and not too fast, with the tailer watching the sail to ensure he does not pull the clew in hard while the leech is still inside the shrouds and spreaders.

In this situation, the mainsail trimmer will have eased the sheet before the tack to increase boat speed and the traveller must be pulled to windward as the boat starts her turn.Then, as she bears away on the new tack, it must be pulled high on the new windward side. As usual, the mainsheet can be trimmed in to its 'proper' position as speed builds and the traveller eased to keep the boom just on the centreline. Initially, the genoa should be sheeted so that it is only just inside the guard-rails and only brought in fully as speed builds. If you have genoa car pullers it may be worth easing the sheet-lead forward as the sheet is eased coming into the tack. This will help to keep the leech under control. As speed builds after the tack, the lead can be pulled aft again. (See Illustration 1.2)

Tacking – Heavy Weather

Tacking in heavy weather with a small jib needs a different technique again. Here, not being stopped by waves and not allowing the boat to heel too much either before or after the tack are probably the most important considerations. I recall one tack I did in the dark and thirty miles from land in a lightweight ten-metre yacht. Everyone was hiking hard and as 'ready about' was called the whole, relatively inexperienced crew, shuffled the bodies in a bit and at least three people got off the rail to prepare for their jobs. At the same time a gust hit us and the yacht just broached to windward and capsized like a dinghy. A few seconds of excitement later, she came upright again but with a very wet topmast and no Windex left! Keep the crew sitting out as long as possible and be prepared to feather into the wind once anyone is off the rail.

On another occasion, we had just tacked when we were hit by a gust before the crew had time to arrive on the weather rail. Without the crew sitting out the yacht broached, the helmsman was not ready, the mainsheet trimmer had the traveller too far to windward and we broach tacked again – not a fast way to sail.

You do need to give your crew a bit more time to get ready than in normal conditions and it is likely that at least one more person will need to be off the rail as soon as 'ready about' is called. The runners will now be critical, so someone must be ready to tend them. Also the yacht will tend to tack much faster in a strong wind and with a small jib, so the rest of the crew will need sufficient warning to prepare to change sides fast as soon as the yacht starts to turn.

1. At 'ready about' – trimmer, runner man and possibly the winch grinder leave the rail – the helmsman feathers the yacht into the wind to stop her heeling excessively.

2. Positive 'ready' from the crew. Delays are more likely in heavy weather and mistakes are much more costly.

3. 'Lee-ho' – helm over. Jib sheet let fly and immediately tailed and wound in hard on the new side. Bowman ready to skirt but will probably not be needed.

4. As the boat bears away the helmsman must keep the boat feathered on the new tack until the crew weight is on the rail. The main traveller should be dropped to the leeward end of the track and only slowly pulled up as the yacht settles on the new tack – too high initially and a windward broach is likely.

5. The jib is trimmed in almost all the way and as soon as the yacht has regained speed, which should be quite quickly, the last few centimetres are wound in, the sheet cleated and the trimmer moves to the windward side.

Reefing

The principle of slab reefing is straightforward enough. All you are doing is taking a horizontal piece out of the foot of the sail by lowering the halyard and pulling down at luff and leech. Once again, in practice there are a few important points to take into account.

A. Laminated or Kevlar sails do not like to flap and it is vital that the sail should only do so for the shortest time possible.

B. The reefing line at the clew will always have one component pulling the leech down and another pulling the sail out along the boom. This means that it is important not to have tension on the reefing line until the halyard is fully hoisted because otherwise there is a very real risk of ripping the sail out of the luff track.

C. The halyard and reefing lines should all be marked clearly so that the sail can be dropped quickly to its mark for each reef and the reef lines can be wound straight in without the need to be continually watching the end of the boom.

The procedure for putting in a reef will go something like the following:-

1. One person off the rail to prepare. Get the reefing line on its winch, get the main halyard ready to drop and a handle ready to wind it back up again. Release the kicking strap.

2. Second person off the rail – to the mast ready to pull the luff down and hook it on at the tack reefing cringle.

3. Drop the halyard to the appropriate mark, pull the sail down by the luff and hook on the reef tack. (NB. The helmsman will experience lee helm at this stage so he must be prepared for this and should keep steering on the genoa tell-tales).

Photo1.5 Once the sail is lowered sufficiently, the reef tack is slipped over the horn and then the halyard is tensioned.

4. Re-tension the main halyard.

5. Pull the slack out of the reefing line and wind it in to its mark. As this happens the mainsheet trimmer should totally release his sheet. The trimmer can watch the end of the boom to ensure the sail is not getting snagged in the reef line etc.

6. Sheet in, kicking strap on and tidy up. The tidying up might include putting coloured

sail-ties fairly loosely around the sail through the eyelets provided in the sail. In rough weather it is worth considering putting a safety lashing through the clew cringle and around the boom – just in case the reef line were to break.

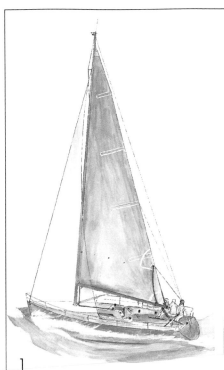

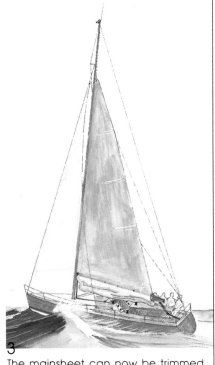

1

It is prudent to have your reefing line rigged if there is heavy weather forecast. Here the red reef line can be seen running from the boom to the reef clew on the leech of the mainsail.

One crew should position the reef line on its winch and prepare the main halyard so that it can be dropped, with a winch handle ready for it to be re-tensioned. Another crew should be at the mast ready to pull down the luff of the mainsail and secure the reef tack over the horn at the goose-neck.

Remember — when you start thinking about putting in a reef, that is the time to do it. Leave it too late, and the boat will become unstable and the task more difficult.

2

The main halyard is dropped cleanly to the position of the reef. Do not feed it, as that makes life difficult for the mast-man. The mainsheet is eased and kicking-strap released. When the reef tack is secure re-tension the main halyard.

Now the reef line is pulled in, thus bringing the reef clew down to the boom. As in all cases when using a winch, watch the results of your efforts — not the winch — when the foot looks tight the reef line should be secured.

Fig 1.3 Slab Reefing

3

The mainsheet can now be trimmed and the kicking-strap applied.

If the situation means that the reef is only likely to be kept in for a reasonably short time, such as in a squall or on the final stages of a short windward leg, then it is not worth tidying up the redundant sail under the boom. If however it looks like being a prolonged blow with the likelihood of green water sweeping the decks, or if you have put in two or more reefs, then you should run a line through the reef eyelets to tidy up the sail and keep it clear of the deck and rogue seas.

All ladies and gentlemen should then retire to the weather rail to enjoy the delights of mother nature.

Shaking Out a Reef

Taking a reef out is basically the reverse of putting one in. The same criteria apply in that the sail must flap for as little as possible and the tension must be released from the reefing line before the luff of the sail is slackened. As before, being prepared in advance of doing anything to effect the sail is vital.

The sequence is:-

1. One person off the rail to prepare. Flake out the working reefing line and any others that are rove. Prepare the main halyard so that it can be dropped twenty centimetres and then re-hoisted and release the kicking strap. Also remove any sail-ties and safety lashings from the sail.

2. Second person off the rail goes to the mast.

3. Release the reef line completely.

4. Lower the halyard enough to unhook the reef tack.

5. Hoist the main halyard with the crew at the mast feeding the sail into the luff groove. NB. Since you will have over a metre of halyard to hoist, it can often be worth passing the tail to another crew member who is still on the rail. While the sail is being hoisted the mainsheet will need to be released.

6. Kicking strap back on, sheet in and crew back on the rail as quickly as possible.

Headsail Changes – General

Every time you change a headsail while the sail is set there will be some general points which apply regardless of what type of change you are undertaking.

Halyards must remain untwisted at the masthead. This is just a housekeeping responsibility but must always be kept in mind.

The new sail will almost certainly have a different sheeting position to the old one and the new sheet must have its lead adjusted before the new sail is hoisted.

To make changes easier, the sails should always be packed in their bags so that the whole luff is flaked together and is readily accessible. The flaked luff should also be tied securely with a sail-tie so that it does not blow apart once the bag has been removed.

Only crew who are essential for the change should come off the rail. Remember that each additional crew coming off the rail will slow the boat progressively.

Genoa Tack Change

When beating to windward and a headsail change is required, a tack change is always the preferred option whenever possible. You will need the windward luff groove to be free and to be able to tack from a tactical point of view. The advantage of a tack change over a straight line change is two-fold. First it is safe and easy to do since the new sail is hoisted on the existing windward side, then the yacht tacks and the old sail is dropped on the new windward side. Secondly, there is minimum loss of speed because crew only remain on the foredeck for a short time and the two sails' interference with each other lasts for less time.

The sequence of operations is as follows:-

1. One crew member gets the new sail on deck and passes it to the bowman. Meanwhile the bowman gets the windward halyard ready.

2. The bowman clips the halyard onto the head of the new sail and takes the sail (in its bag) forward, attaches the tack and feeds the head through the pre-feeder and into the luff groove. (See Photo 1.6)

3. The trimmer unclips the lazy sheet from the old sail, adjusts the sheet lead for the new sail and releads the sheet as necessary, then clips the lazy sheet onto the new sail.

4. The pitman starts to hoist the new sail (Photo 1.7) and when it is almost at the top the helmsman commences the tack. During the tack, the pitman completes hoisting the new sail and releases the old sail's halyard.

5. The cockpit crew tack as normal (onto the new sail) and the bowman pulls down the old sail, detaches the tack and drags the sail off the foredeck as quickly as possible. (See Photos 1.8 & 1.9)

6. The old halyard is unclipped and restowed at the mast, the second sheet is taken off the old sail, re-led as necessary and attached to the new sail. The old sail is flaked roughly and stowed in its bag.

7. All crew except the trimmer resume their positions on the rail, the trimmer looks at the shape of the new sail and adjusts the halyard and sheet lead if required.

Photo 1.6 The bowman has attached the tack of the new sail and is inserting the head into the luff groove. Note the boat is on starboard tack.

Photo 1.7 The new sail is on its way up. The bowman watches to see that the luff runs smoothly and that nothing jams in the pre-feeder. The mastman is sweating the halyard at the mast and the pitman will be tailing flat-out with the rope around a winch. The boat still sails on starboard tack.

Photo 1.8 → Here the boat is tacking onto port. The new sail has been fully hoisted and already the bowman is pulling the luff of the redundant sail to get it down and cleared away as fast as possible.

Photo 1.9 Now sailing on port tack, the old sail has almost been lowered. The bowman is still pulling the sail down at the luff (the correct method which causes no harm to the sail) while the sweeper gathers the body of the sail to keep it under control and stop it sliding over the side.

Fig 1.4 Headsail Tack Change

2

The boat has tacked and the old sail is being lowered inside the smaller new sail which is now powering the boat.

The sheet from the lowered sail will be re-attached to the new sail as a priority, and at the same time the windward fairlead should be moved accordingly.

All that remains is for the bowman to clear the old sail from the foredeck and to bring its halyard back to the mast.

1

The new smaller headsail has been hoisted as the call 'Ready About' is given. The bowman will be ready near the bow so that he can swing round the forestay and start pulling down the luff of the redundant, larger sail as soon as the boat has tacked through the wind.

Note that the sheet has been attached to the new sail and that the fairlead position will have been adjusted to accommodate the new sail when the boat has tacked.

One crew member remains in the companionway ready to release the halyard of what will become the old sail.

Genoa Change
– Straight Line – Inside Set

When you have to change headsails and the windward groove is free but for some reason you are unable to tack, then you need to make a straight line, inside set type of change.

This is slightly harder than a tack change for two reasons. Firstly, you will need to reeve a spare sheet and secondly, the old sail will come down to leeward of the new one and it may be necessary to have two people on the foredeck to retrieve it quickly and safely. Also, if the new sail is larger and overlaps the old one by any great degree, it may be difficult to set the new sail inside. This is particularly true if the old sail sheets inside the shrouds and the new one sheets outside. In this latter case it may be quickest to put a temporary sheet onto the old non-overlapping sail on the outside track before commencing the change.

The sequence starts in much the same way as a tack change.

1. The new sail is brought on deck and it, together with the windward halyard is taken forward and plugged into the pre-feeder and headfoil.

2. The trimmer gets a spare sheet and reeves it as appropriate for the new sail. Alternatively, he may have to rig a short change-sheet onto the old sail if the same genoa-car is needed for the new sail. This will allow the sheet lead to be correct as soon as the new sail is hoisted.

3. The lazy sheet is taken off the old sail, re-led and attached to the new sail.

4. The new headsail is hoisted and the halyard wound to its mark.

5. The new sail is sheeted in and the sheet released from the old one.

6. The old sail is dropped (for this to happen smoothly the halyard for the old sail must have been flaked beforehand). As the old sail comes down, the bowman will need to be right forward, pulling it out of the headfoil with another crewman pulling the bundle of sail under the new genoa and up to the windward side. It can help considerably if the tack of the old sail is released as soon as the halyard comes slack because it is then possible to drag the whole sail away from the bow as it comes down.

7. The old sail is flaked and bagged (or stuffed below) and the job is done.

1

In this example the boat is changing down from a genoa to a smaller blade-jib.

At this stage the blade has been hoisted and its sheet (shown in red) attached and run through the correct fairlead. The larger sail is still powering the yacht.

The crew in the companionway is ready to release the genoa halyard and the bowman will be positioned near the pulpit ready to release the tack of the redundant sail and pull it down under the foot of the new jib.

2

The genoa halyard has been released and the bowman is clawing at the luff of the old sail to get it down as soon as possible.

The genoa sheet has been removed so that the entire sail can be gathered up onto the windward side of the foredeck under the foot of the jib. Sometimes if both sails have become soaked with spray they tend to stick together and the friction that is created makes life difficult for the bowman. A kindly helmsman will give a quick luff if he sees this situation developing — the shimmer of the sails as he does this will break them apart and the old sail should descend rapidly.

Fig 1.5 Straight Line Headsail Change — Inside Set

Genoa Change
– Straight Line – Outside Set

As its name suggests, this is the manoeuvre which is necessary when you wish to change genoas and the leeward groove and halyard are free. Unless the old sail is fitted with a luff Cunningham that would allow the sail to be released from the tack fitting and thus provide a slot under it for hoisting the new sail, the chief problem associated with this hoist is the physical difficulty of feeding the new sail under the foot of the old one and between it and the guard-rails.

Associated problems are; twisting the head of the sail as it is fed under the old sail and having the new sail washed aft by waves as it is fed under the foot of the old sail.

1. Preparation is virtually the same as for an inside set, except that the halyard will need to be taken around the leeward side of the old genoa on its way to the bow. The new sail needs to be brought on deck and taken forward, a change-sheet needs to be rove and the lazy sheet should come off the old sail and be bent on to the new one.

2. The sail must be flaked so that the whole luff is together and the bag needs to be pulled right forward, to within twenty to thirty centimetres of the tack fitting. The bowman then takes the head of the new sail under the foot of the old genoa and feeds it through the pre-feeder and into the headfoil. He then attaches the halyard.

3. The mastman carefully sweats up the new sail while the bowman pulls it under the old genoa and feeds it into the pre-feeder and headfoil. The bowman will be working from within the pulpit, leaning around to the leeward side of the old sail. He should attach the tack when the sail is almost hoisted.

4. Once the sail is fully hoisted and the halyard is at its mark, the new sail is sheeted in and the old sheet is cast off. At this time the old sail is pulled down in exactly the same manner as in a tack change.

If the new genoa is allowed to blow or get washed backwards while it is being hoisted, there is a real danger of it pulling out of the pre-feeder and then out of the headfoil. This is why the mastman must sweat the new halyard up carefully, watching the bowman as he does so. If the sail does come out of the headfoil, there is no option other than to pull it down and start again.

Photo 1.11 The bowman stays in the pulpit to help the luff into the luff groove as the sail is hoisted.

←**Photo 1.10** Here the bowman has taken the head of the sail to be hoisted under the foot of the working sail and is inserting it into the leeward luff groove. The new sail lies in its bag between the foot of the working sail and the guard-rail.

Packing a Genoa
– On the Side-deck

If genoas have been changed while sailing upwind and if there is still a fair distance to go before the next mark or the finish, the old sail will need to be re-packed with as little disruption as possible. In light airs it may be best to take it below and pack it, but in most cases it will be more efficient to do the packing on the windward side-deck.

The exact technique will vary according to the yacht and the conditions but some general rules apply in most cases.

1. The luff should be flaked first with the leech being flaked independently a little behind.

2. The luff should be upwind – at the front if you are going to windward. This enables the wind to do some of your work for you and blow the rest of the sail back and into some semblance of shape.

3. Crew weight should be kept as far outboard as possible. It is often possible to flake the sail with everyone on the rail but shuffled in a few centimetres, with the sail on the laps of the crew. If this is not feasible, only the minimum crew to do the job should be off the rail.

4. Don't try to do a perfect shore-side type of flake. So long as the luff is together, the sail is untwisted and it fits into its sausage bag then no more neatness is required.

5. Remember to fasten a sail tie tightly around the luff before bagging the sail. This makes life much easier for the bowman when the sail is needed next.

6. Put the sail in the correct bag! This sounds obvious but since this is one of the few times you will have a choice of two sailbags it is amazingly easy to make a mistake.

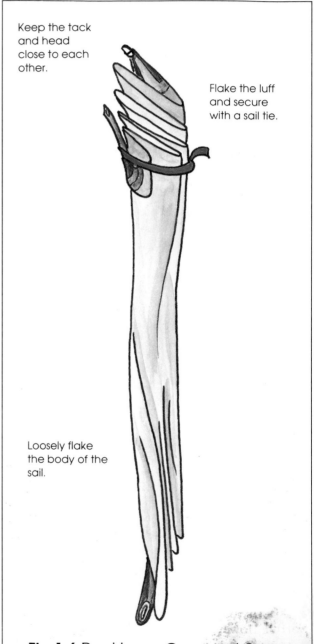

Keep the tack and head close to each other.

Flake the luff and secure with a sail tie.

Loosely flake the body of the sail.

Fig 1.6 Packing a Genoa at Sea

Photo 1.12 Packing a headsail on the windward side-deck. The crew are trying to keep their weight as far to windward as they can. Do not seek the perfection of a more leisurely fold made ashore or below decks.

Spinnaker Hoists
– General Points

As with most manoeuvres, hoisting a spinnaker quickly and efficiently is mainly a matter of being prepared and having gear which works properly. There are many techniques that can be used in differing conditions and some of these will be dealt with shortly. However before looking at the specific techniques it is worthwhile to examine some of the basic requirements in detail.

Until the spinnaker is up and setting, the genoa will be providing the driving force and so it needs to be trimmed properly. The only time that this will not be true is if you are bearing away sharply and are going to hoist the spinnaker as you bear away. In this case, the genoa will simply need to be eased slightly to enable the mainsail to be dumped in the bear away, accurate trimming will not be needed and may even be detrimental to a good set. Obviously if there is a delay between bearing away and getting the spinnaker up, the genoa must be trimmed.

The sail nearly always needs to go up as fast as possible and this means having the halyard led in such a way that it can be pulled up quickly – normally a mast exit at about two metres above the deck is utilised so that the mastman can sweat the sail to the top with the halyard or pitman just tailing the slack. Once the spinnaker sets, there will suddenly be a lot of pressure in the halyard and if the mastman is not to be pulled into the mast, the tail of the halyard must be led either through a stopper or round a winch.

If the layout of the yacht precludes having a mast exit at or above head height and the halyards come out of the base of the mast, the main pull on the halyard should be on a bight of the rope as it goes along the deck – being careful not to pull directly from the forward side of a winch or else you are bound to get riding turns.

The sail must be packed in such a way that it is unlikely to twist as it goes up. In most situations this will be helped if the tack of the sail is pulled towards the pole end as the sail starts to go up, probably getting the tack as far as the forestay initially, before squaring it fully once the sail is almost at the top.

In anything other than very light conditions it is not sensible to set the spinnaker until it has reached the top or else it is going to be very hard to pull or wind the halyard the last few metres. Thus the sheet should not be trimmed on until the sail is at or near the top, except perhaps for a brief sheet on just to spread the foot out as it comes out of the bag, before dumping the sheet again. Once again, this can help to prevent twists. With large spinnakers and especially those used in strong winds, it may well be worth putting rubber bands or wool stoppers around the sail every metre or so to allow the sail to be fully hoisted before it tries to fill.

The pole will need to be raised to approximately the correct height before the guy is squared or else the downward pull of the guy will work directly against the less powerful uphaul (topping lift) and may well prevent the pole being raised.

Most spinnaker hoists are straightforward bear away sets or sets from a close reach. In both of these situations it is far easier for the mastman to work on the windward side. It is also normally best to use the leeward halyard for the first hoist since this allows one inside spinnaker peel without twisting halyards thus it is often best to cross the halyards inside the mast, so that the port halyard at the top comes out of the starboard side at the bottom and vice versa.

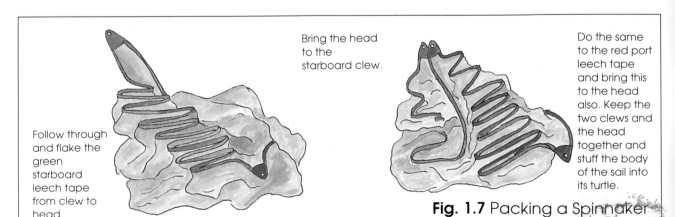

Follow through and flake the green starboard leech tape from clew to head.

Bring the head to the starboard clew.

Do the same to the red port leech tape and bring this to the head also. Keep the two clews and the head together and stuff the body of the sail into its turtle.

Fig. 1.7 Packing a Spinnaker

Spinnaker Hoist
– Bear Away Set

As already stated, the bear away set will be the most common type of hoist you are likely to make. With adequate preparation it should be an easy set in all but the windiest of conditions, but like any other manoeuvre it can just as easily go wrong unless all the crew know what to do.

For this type of set, the sail can be placed virtually anywhere from the pulpit back to the mast. The only real disadvantage of having it well forward is the necessity of having the bowman up at the very end of the boat to clip it on. As a general rule, you should have the bag progressively further forward as the wind comes aft, although as already implied this is not critical.

When beating up to a windward mark, it obviously makes sense to time the set up so that as much work as possible is done on the windward side. This often means it is best to set the pole up on the tack you intend to hoist and to set the spinnaker itself when you are on the other tack, thus enabling all work to be done from the windward side.

The sequence of operations for the set up will vary slightly according to the point of sailing you are on at the time and as to whether you need to tack again before hoisting, but in general it will go as follows:-

1. Cockpit crew take knots out of the sheets and guys and pull them around so that the snap shackles are located correctly on the foredeck.

Photo 1.13 The sheet and guy (also halyard here) are pulled to the launch position.

Photo 1.14 The bowman places the guy into the beak of the spinnaker pole.

3. Bowman checks/clips on the pole topping lift. If you need to tack again before hoisting, a bight of the topping lift should be taken back to the mast and held there temporarily until after the final tack.

4. The bowman gets the spinnaker halyard and clips it to the same place as the sheets and guys. If using the leeward halyard at the masthead, this will need to be taken to leeward of the genoa before the hoist. If this is done on the opposite tack to that for the hoist itself, then the halyard should be able to be taken directly from the mast to the foredeck. However if the halyard is taken forward while on the same tack as the hoist, it can be quite awkward to get the halyard around the back of the genoa, along the side-deck, and running outside the genoa, especially if it is a wire halyard that will not easily bend around the foot of the genoa. A simple trick to help this operation is to clip a sail tie onto the snapshackle, leave the complete halyard to leeward of the genoa and pull it around using the sail tie.

5. Sewer rat crew gets the spinnaker bag and passes it to either the mastman or the bowman for taking forward and clipping on. Once again it is easier if this is done while on the opposite tack to the hoist.

6. The bowman takes the bag forward, clips it to the guard-rails and then clips the sheets and guys to the tack and clew of the spinnaker, taking care not to put twists into the sail. If close to the hoist, this is also the time to clip on the halyard but if not, it may be worth leaving the halyard until a little later.

2. Bowman ensures the outboard end of the spinnaker pole is on the correct side of the forestay (and if relevant, that the pole is on the correct side of the babystay). At the same time, he clips the guy into the beak of the pole. (See Photo 1.14)

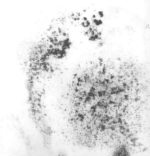

Normally the bag will be attached to the side which will be to leeward during the hoist but in very rough seas there is a real risk of the spinnaker being washed out of the bag before it is hoisted. In these circumstances and assuming your foredeck is virtually devoid of sharp snags such as cleats etc., it can be a good idea to attach the bag onto the windward side, pull the sheets, guys and halyard under the foot of the genoa and under the spinnaker pole up to the spinnaker. When the sail is then hoisted it will go up as normal but from the windward side of the foredeck instead of the more usual leeward side.

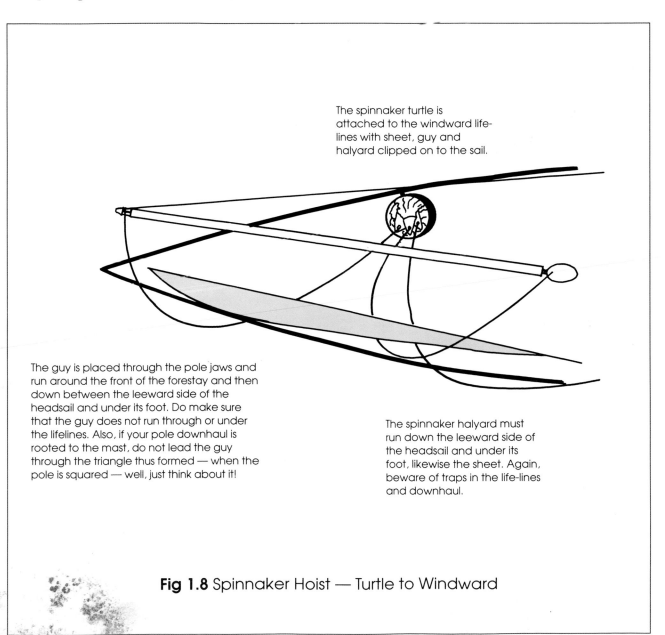

The spinnaker turtle is attached to the windward life-lines with sheet, guy and halyard clipped on to the sail.

The guy is placed through the pole jaws and run around the front of the forestay and then down between the leeward side of the headsail and under its foot. Do make sure that the guy does not run through or under the lifelines. Also, if your pole downhaul is rooted to the mast, do not lead the guy through the triangle thus formed — when the pole is squared — well, just think about it!

The spinnaker halyard must run down the leeward side of the headsail and under its foot, likewise the sheet. Again, beware of traps in the life-lines and downhaul.

Fig 1.8 Spinnaker Hoist — Turtle to Windward

7. The mastman can get the inboard end of the pole set to the correct height even if there is still another tack to make before the hoist.

8. Once on the final approach to the hoist, the pole should be topped and the top of the bag opened if not done already.
(See Photo 1.15)

9. As you start to bear away for the hoist, the spinnaker guy should be squared slightly, until the tack of the sail is at the pole end with the pole just clear of the forestay – this helps to stop the sail wrapping around itself. The genoa sheet needs to be eased slightly and then cleated. The mastman sweats the halyard up as fast as possible while the pitman keeps up with his tailing. (See Photo1.16)

Photo 1.15 The pole has been topped. The mastman is ready for the hoist and the pitman is waiting to tail the halyard around the winch. The guy also is around a winch with two crew ready for the initial jerk to get the clew from the bag to the end of the pole, one for tailing and another ready on the winch. Hopefully the bowman will remember to open the bag!

Photo 1.16 → The guy has already pulled the spinnaker clew out to the pole. The mastman is giving the halyard his all – but the trimmer waits to sheet-in until the sail is at full hoist.

10. As the spinnaker goes up, the guy should be squared back so that as the spinnaker reaches the top, the pole is positioned correctly.

11. As the spinnaker hits the top, the genoa halyard should be dropped and the spinnaker sheet pulled in until the sail fills. It may be necessary to bear away a little below the proper course to get the sail to fill when on a close reach, but be careful not to overdo this. The reason for dropping the genoa immediately is similar in that the air that was going around the headsail is suddenly released into the top of the spinnaker and helps dramatically in achieving a quick set.

Photo 1.17 Full hoist, sheet coming on and headsail on the way down.

Fig 1.9 Spinnaker Hoist
— Bear Away Set

1

On the final approach to the mark, this boat has the pole set to the correct height with the guy (red line) through the beak and the lazy spinnaker sheet (pink) resting on the pole end. The spinnaker turtle is to leeward of the headsail and ready to go. The blue line is the lazy headsail sheet which runs in front of the pole topping lift.

2

As the boat rounds the mark the mastman sweats the spinnaker halyard up, the guy is pulling the spinnaker to the pole end and the foredeck crew is helping the kite out of its bag. It is helpful if the headsail trimmer does not ease his sheet fully, but only out to a reaching trim; in this way there is less interference to the spinnaker's upwards progress through friction with the genoa.

3

With the kite up and pulling the sheet trimmer has taken to the weather deck so that he has a clear view of the sail. The headsail is almost down and will be made secure on deck. The bowman will get his weight off the foredeck as quickly as he can.

12. The genoa is pulled down, taking care not to let it wash over the side. It will then either be very roughly stowed on the foredeck, with just a sail tie around the luff or it will be taken off the foredeck for re-bagging if there is a chance that a different genoa will be needed on the next upwind leg.

13. Once the spinnaker is up and set properly, the next thing to concentrate on is getting the rig and mainsail set properly. The mainsail controls (clew outhaul and halyard) need to be eased, the vang should be adjusted for optimum leech tension and the sheet eased until the mainsail is either against the shrouds or is just about luffing.

If the wind is abaft the beam, the head of the mast should be taken forward by attaching the genoa halyard to the tack fitting and winding the mast forward whilst easing out the backstay and runners. Be careful while winding the mast forward not to overdo it and invert the mast. Unless you have a load gauge on the front of the mast to measure when it is straight, someone should be sighting up the mast to ensure that the rig is as far forward as possible but is still either straight or curved slightly back at the top.

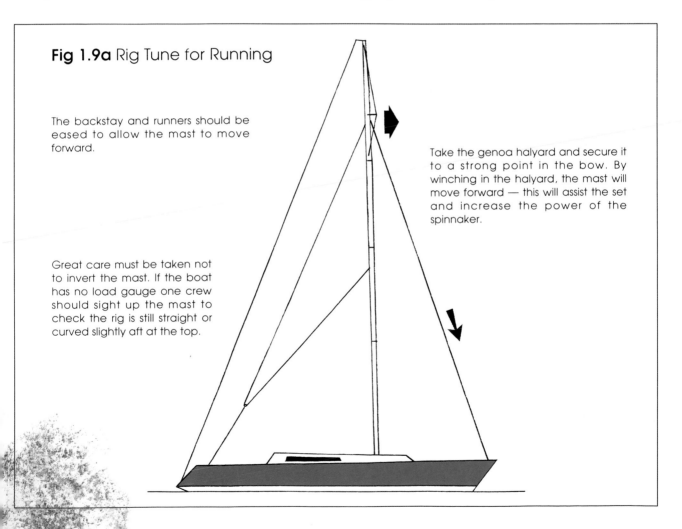

Fig 1.9a Rig Tune for Running

The backstay and runners should be eased to allow the mast to move forward.

Take the genoa halyard and secure it to a strong point in the bow. By winching in the halyard, the mast will move forward — this will assist the set and increase the power of the spinnaker.

Great care must be taken not to invert the mast. If the boat has no load gauge one crew should sight up the mast to check the rig is still straight or curved slightly aft at the top.

Spinnaker Hoist
– Gybe Set

The gybe set is used when you approach a mark and must gybe around it in order to sail the correct (or optimum) course and also need to hoist the spinnaker at the same time. The manoeuvre will never be used in very light airs because it is unlikely the spinnaker will set properly while going dead downwind and so a bear away set followed by a gybe will nearly always be quicker when the wind is light. Only the very best crews would attempt a gybe set in really windy conditions because the potential for drama is quite high!

The principle of the gybe set is very simple. As you bear away onto a run, before you actually gybe, up goes the spinnaker and sets just on the sheets. Once the genoa has been gybed, you top the pole, square back the guy and away you go – no problem at all.

The practice is not much more difficult but for the set to be a success you do need to be well prepared and there are a few common errors that need to be eliminated if the whole thing is not to end in tears.

1. Preparation is more or less the same as for a bear away set. The differences are:-

a) The spinnaker bag should be placed as far forward as possible to minimise interference with the genoa.

b) If the pole topping lift's mast exit is high enough, the pole hoist will be speeded up a little if the topping lift is taken from the mast exit, around the leeward side of the genoa and brought in under the foot of the genoa before being attached to the end of the pole. This enables the pole to be topped as soon as the genoa itself has been gybed and avoids having to wait for sufficient slackening in the genoa sheet.

c) Obviously, the bag and the pole need to be set for the side that will be correct once the gybe has been completed; that is with the pole to leeward on your final approach to the mark.

2. As you approach the mark, the bowman should go forward to help the spinnaker out of the bag and to ensure that the genoa does not get snagged on the end of the pole during the gybe. Cockpit crew prepare as for a bear away hoist except that the mainsheet trimmer will initially let his sheet out to allow the boat to bear away before pulling it across in the gybe. Also, the genoa trimmer must gybe the genoa across, having also eased his sheet a little on the bear away.

3. Once the wind is abaft the beam the spinnaker can start to go up – as fast as possible, with both clews being pulled aft using the sheets – ideally to pre-marked running positions. As the spinnaker reaches the top it should be set without the pole for a short time.

4. Once the genoa has been gybed across, the pole is topped and then the guy brought back and the spinnaker set as normal. One of the most common mistakes is to be lax about gybing the genoa, thinking that since it is about to be dropped, it does not matter. In fact, unless it is gybed across quickly and sheeted in at least half way it will always snag either the pole end (preventing it from being topped) or the leeward spinnaker clew and sheet (preventing the sail from setting).

5. As the spinnaker halyard reaches the top, or even a second before, the genoa halyard should be cast off – as before, this will allow wind to fill the spinnaker and thus help it to set.

6. Remaining sequence as bear away set.

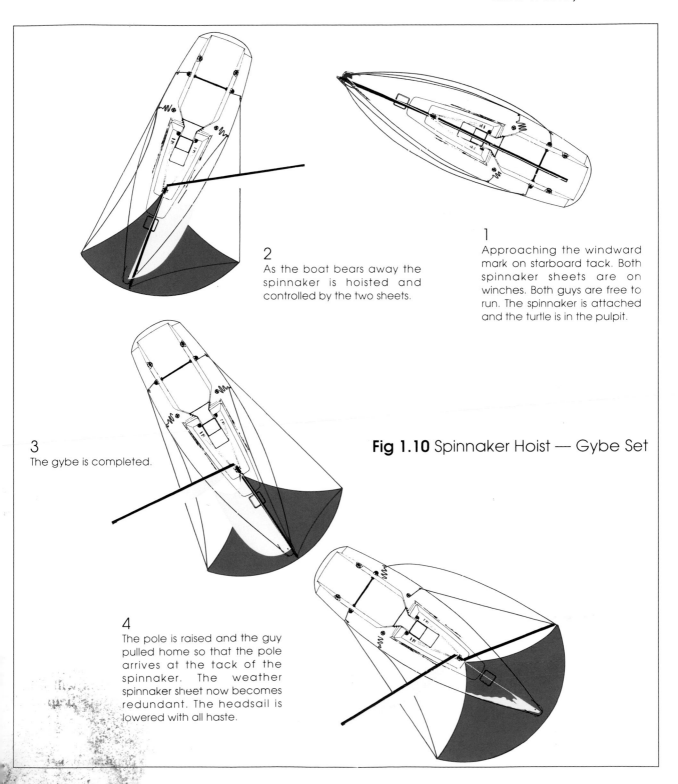

2
As the boat bears away the spinnaker is hoisted and controlled by the two sheets.

1
Approaching the windward mark on starboard tack. Both spinnaker sheets are on winches. Both guys are free to run. The spinnaker is attached and the turtle is in the pulpit.

3
The gybe is completed.

Fig 1.10 Spinnaker Hoist — Gybe Set

4
The pole is raised and the guy pulled home so that the pole arrives at the tack of the spinnaker. The weather spinnaker sheet now becomes redundant. The headsail is lowered with all haste.

Spinnaker Hoist – Tack set

It sometimes happens that it is necessary to approach a mark and make a close-hauled tack for a very short time before bearing away sufficiently to hoist the spinnaker.

When this is the case, set up the spinnaker to windward, with sheet, guy and halyard clipped on and guy through the pole end. Raise the pole at the mast end and leave enough slack in the pole downhaul to enable it to be raised to its working height. The bowman should take the pole uphaul under the lazy headsail sheet before clipping it to the pole, and at the same time make sure that the outer pole end is to windward of the forestay. He should then take a bight of the slack pole uphaul back to the mast and either clip it to the mast or hold it until the headsail has been tacked. The headsail should run over the top of the pole during the tack but may need assistance from the bowman or his helper. Once close hauled after the tack, the pole can be raised and the normal sequence for a bear away set should follow.

Gybing Symmetrical Spinnakers – General Points

Gybing with a spinnaker set is probably the manoeuvre which causes more difficulties than any other. Watching a top crew gybe is a delight and makes one realise that it does not need to cause difficulties if you are well prepared and understand what is happening.

During most gybes, the feeling is always very much that the bowman is in control and that if anything goes wrong it is his fault. In reality it is usually the helmsman who is (or should be) in control and he is the one who makes it look easy or ends up with a mess. Obviously, the whole crew need to work in harmony and any one of the crew can screw up and make the gybe more difficult, but in general – blame the helm if you end up broaching or with the spinnaker wrapped around the forestay! The helmsman must be able to steer the yacht under the spinnaker and needs a good feel of when he has real control for initiating the manoeuvre.

The most critical time in any gybe is the moment when the spinnaker is tripped from the pole so that it flies free on the sheets. This is when the spinnaker can take control of the boat with a wild gyration, so before tripping the pole, not only must the helmsman be ready but also the trimmer(s) should have the spinnaker totally under control on the sheets.

In order to let the whole crew feel happy at gybing, it can be of great assistance to practise sailing without a pole. Try sailing on a squarish run with the spinnaker set as normal and then trip the pole away as if you were going to gybe. Now simply sail the yacht under the spinnaker, trimming if necessary with the two sheets and once settled, top the pole and square the guy again before tripping the pole away once more. After practising on a square run until really confident, try altering course gently both ways so that you see what happens and what is needed if you are sailing by the lee or are forced to luff slightly. Practising in this way will give everyone on the yacht the feel of how to control and play the spinnaker during a gybe, even if something goes wrong in the middle of the manoeuvre and it takes longer than anticipated. Obviously this practise should be started in easy, moderate conditions and only when that seems simple should it be tried in more testing conditions.

Keeping the spinnaker full during a gybe should always be the aim. In light weather your speed will plummet if the spinnaker collapses and in windy conditions there is the real danger of bursting the spinnaker as it refills once having been allowed to collapse. Having said that, there will be times, especially inshore, when getting the yacht around the mark inside a competitor takes priority over everything else, but usually keeping the spinnaker full is paramount.

Spinnaker Gybing – Dip Pole – Run to Run in Moderate Weather

Gybing in moderate weather should not present any real problems. The spinnaker will fly quite happily and there should not be difficulty with control of the yacht. Gybing from run to run is the simplest since the pole will already be quite square before the manoeuvre starts.

The sequence will go something like the following:-

1. Command 'Prepare to Gybe'. Crew move to their positions. Lazy guy has half a turn put around its winch, and the bowman takes a bight of the lazy guy and then stands in readiness just forward of the mast until the manoeuvre commences. If the pole tripping line is led through a block halfway along the pole so that the bowman can trip the old guy himself, then he also gets hold of the tripping line. The lazy sheet is loaded onto its winch and the slack removed. The runners are prepared with the new runner being loaded onto the winch and a handle placed in the top and the old runner flaked ready so that it will run out freely after the gybe. The mainsheet trimmer cleats the traveller amidships and gets ready to either swing the boom straight across or to pull the sheet into the middle depending on the strength of the wind. The pole is adjusted on the mast to the correct height and the topping lift is prepared for lowering. (NB. If the topping lift has a cleat at the mast as well as a cleat and/or a winch further aft, it can be cleated at the mast and just enough slack put between there and the cleat aft so that in the gybe, it may be dropped out of the mast cleat to fall automatically to the right height.)

2. The helmsman sees that all is ready, calls 'bearing away' and starts to bear away further. As he commences the move, the bowman runs forward, still with the bight of the lazy guy and the tripping line in his hands. The new sheet is further tensioned to take most of the weight off the old guy and the old sheet is eased a little. If the mainsail needs sheeting into the middle, the trimmer works as fast as possible to pull it in, otherwise he waits until the yacht is by the lee before pulling the sail across in one go.

3. Just before the yacht is by the lee, the helmsman shouts 'trip'. At this call, the bowman (or mastman if the tripping line exits the pole by the mast) trips the pole end to release the old guy and at the same time the mastman quickly lowers the topping lift to the prearranged mark so that the pole drops into the hands of the bowman.

4. As the main boom swings across the centreline, the new runner is tensioned by hand to a safe mark and the old runner is let go. As soon as the old runner is off, the mainsail is let out smoothly on the new side. At the same time, the spinnaker pole is pulled into the centre by the bowman and as it passes him, he puts the lazy guy into the end and closes the jaws – calling 'Made!' as he does so.

5. At the call of 'made' from the bow, the mastman sweats the topping lift to its mark with the pitman tailing, while at the same time the new guy is wound back. These two operations must be carried out together so that the pole goes up and back in a smooth arc. If the pole is topped too quickly there is a danger of putting the end of the pole through the foot of the spinnaker, whereas if the guy is wound back too fast it will be difficult or impossible to top the pole. As the guy is wound back, the old sheet needs to be eased in sympathy to allow the tack of the sail to go forward to the pole end. Good co-ordination between the guy and sheet trimmers is required here or else the spinnaker is likely to jerk forward and collapse.

Photo 1.18 The pole has been tripped from the old guy and the spinnaker is being flown on the sheets alone. The topping lift has been eased to dip the pole low enough to clear the headstay. The bowman uses the downhaul to pull the pole into the pulpit. He has the new guy ready to insert into the beak. It looks as though he will have a slight problem with the genoa sheet that has wrapped itself neatly around the pole end.

Photo 1.19 Before he can insert the new guy into the pole, the genoa sheet must be cleared. As soon as the guy is secure he will call 'Made'.

Photo 1.20 Up and away. The new guy is tensioned and the topping lift is already raising the pole to the correct height. The genoa sheet will eventually fall back to the deck and can be sorted out later; the most important task is to get the pole set – all else can wait.

Spinnaker Gybing – Dip Pole – Reach to Reach in Moderate Weather

Gybing from reach to reach is not very different from the run to run gybe but there are just enough differences to warrant dealing with the manoeuvre separately.

1. All the preparation is as previously explained except that the old guy will need to be squared back as the yacht bears away and so the person on this line needs to be ready.

2. As the helmsman starts to bear away several things must happen at once.

a) The guy in use needs to be wound back to square the pole.

b) The downhaul should be eased as the pole comes aft.

c) The mainsheet should be eased to allow the yacht to bear away.

d) The sheet in use must be eased to keep the spinnaker set correctly.

3. Once squared away and on a run, the manoeuvre proceeds as for a run to run gybe until the call of 'Made' comes from the bowman.

6. Once the gybe is complete, the helmsman can come up to his proper course with the trimmers following the movement of the yacht with their sheets. If the runners are in use the new runner will need to be wound gently to it's position while checking the mast to ensure it has not inverted.

4. When the new guy is in the pole end, the helmsman will continue his turn and start to come up to the new reaching course. The new guy therefore need not be squared too much or the spinnaker will probably collapse. Ideally, the pole should be brought back to the clew of the spinnaker and then let forward again. As

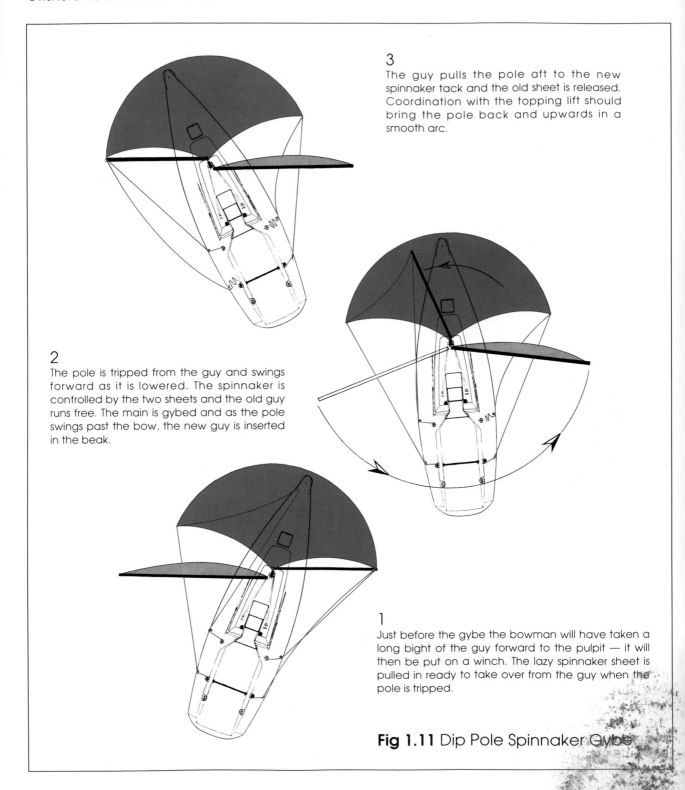

3
The guy pulls the pole aft to the new spinnaker tack and the old sheet is released. Coordination with the topping lift should bring the pole back and upwards in a smooth arc.

2
The pole is tripped from the guy and swings forward as it is lowered. The spinnaker is controlled by the two sheets and the old guy runs free. The main is gybed and as the pole swings past the bow, the new guy is inserted in the beak.

1
Just before the gybe the bowman will have taken a long bight of the guy forward to the pulpit — it will then be put on a winch. The lazy spinnaker sheet is pulled in ready to take over from the guy when the pole is tripped.

Fig 1.11 Dip Pole Spinnaker Gybe

the pole comes back, the old sheet is eased to allow the clew to move forward. Once again, good co-ordination between the trimmers is paramount.

5. Attention to the runners is far more important on a reach to reach gybe, with the added problem that the new runner demands fast, critical action. As the boat bears away from a reach and the mainsail is let out, the runner must also be eased out – but then, as soon as you are on a dead run and the main comes amidships, that same runner must be pulled in super-fast while the leeward one is eased.

6. The other aspect of the gybe which is more important is sheer speed. Since the idea is to turn the yacht smoothly from one reach, through dead downwind and onto the opposite reach, the gybe needs to happen in the middle of the turn – without a hitch. If there is a delay in getting the pole transferred from one guy to the other, then the helmsman must be prepared to slow down the turn to take the delay into account.

Spinnaker Gybing – Dip Pole – Heavy Weather

To successfully dip pole gybe in very strong winds the crew's understanding of the principles concerned needs to be good and they should have practised until perfect in less testing conditions. Reach to reach gybing does not come into the equation since to attempt this would almost certainly be a recipe for disaster. If that is what is needed, a boat would normally bear away to a run first, gybe and then carefully come up to the new reaching course.

In most respects there is little difference between moderate airs run to run gybing and the same manoeuvre in strong winds. There is, however, a difference in the way that trivial errors in moderate conditions can become disastrous when a belly full of wind is blowing and big seas are running.

We shall look at the main differences between gybing in moderate and heavy weather and also those areas where the majority of mistakes are likely to happen.

1. You must be on a very broad reach (almost square run) before attempting to start a gybe.

2. When in surfing conditions, you should aim to start and complete the gybe while surfing at maximum speed and if possible also in a lull. In particular, try not to gybe in the middle of a heavy gust and attempt to complete the gybe before the bow buries itself in the wave ahead. (In either of those bad situations, the apparent wind speed will be significantly higher and the gybe will be that much tougher.)

3. The spinnaker needs to be kept well under control at all times. This will mean positioning the old and new sheet leads further forward than usual in order to control the leech and stop too much twist developing. One of the most common errors is to have insufficient tension on the new sheet just before tripping the old guy out from the pole end. The trimmer needs to wind the new sheet back until there is approximately the same load on it as the guy – otherwise the clew of the sail will shoot forward as the guy is tripped and this will cause control problems both with the steering and with the spinnaker itself.

4. The boat should be steered under the spinnaker, especially while it is flying free on the sheets alone. Remember that this involves anticipation – rather like skiing down a mogul slope where you have your feet turning for the next bump before you have cleared the last one – here the helmsman needs to be a second or so ahead. As the spinnaker rolls to starboard,

the boat should already be moving that same way, otherwise the inertia in the yacht and delays between altering the helm and the boat's response will inevitably mean that you get out of synchronization.

5. The mainsail will almost certainly need to be centralised as you gybe to stop it crashing too heavily across from one side to the other. This will be hard physical work and the mainsheet trimmer may need some help on larger yachts. While the main is amidships, it will be generating large amounts of weather helm and if care is not taken could initiate a broach. Therefore, be careful not to centre the sheet too early and only have the main in the middle for the shortest possible time. Let the sheet run as soon as the main has gybed. If for any reason, the main is brought in too early and there is going to be an obvious delay before the gybe, the sheet should be eased out again, even if this means a slight further delay. The mainsheet trimmer should be watching the helm all the time and should recognise when the helmsman has trouble steering.

6. When approaching the leeward mark and needing to gybe for only a short distance, it will often be faster to hoist the genoa before the gybe, carry on somewhat past the layline, drop the spinnaker and then gybe. The extra distance sailed can be more than compensated for by avoiding a broach and the ensuing panic in the short time that remains between the gybe and the mark rounding, when normally the genoa will need hoisting and the spinnaker dropping.

Spinnaker Gybing – Dip Pole – Light Airs

Light airs gybing involves a quite different technique to that used in moderate or windy conditions and is often harder to achieve

successfully. There are obviously not going to be control problems but the main difficulty lies in being forced to sail for a short time dead downwind. To see what happens, try sailing square on a light day while out practising. The spinnaker will almost certainly collapse and boat speed will drop off rapidly. It will then take an age to increase again as you luff to your normal downwind sailing angle.

The solution to the problem is to sail from reach to reach without a pause, keeping the spinnaker full the whole time. To achieve this, the spinnaker will need to be moved bodily from one side to the other during the turn and this requires good crew co-ordination.

As you come into the gybe, the helmsman will commence a smooth bear away. At the same time, the old guy will be squared back and the old sheet eased. The guy must now be tripped from the end of the pole which should be dipped and swung across to the new side as quickly as possible. As the old sheet is eased forwards, one crew member should take hold of the clew of the sail and physically take it forward to the forestay, holding it there while the new guy is put in the end of the pole. Once the new guy is in the pole the guy is tensioned. By this time the helmsman should be swinging the yacht onto her new reaching course so there should be little need for the pole to be squared.

In this type of light airs gybe, the two most important things are for the helmsman to swing from one reach to the next in a smooth arc and for the trimmers to get the spinnaker from one side to the next as quickly as the boat is turning, without letting the sail collapse.

The mainsail must obviously be gybed as well. This should be done gently and by getting hold of the falls of the sheet and handing the main across.

Spinnaker Gybing – End for End

End for end gybing is used primarily on smaller boats, up to about ten or eleven metres overall length. Instead of dipping the pole into the foredeck where the bowman puts the new guy into the jaws, as in a dip pole gybe, the bowman works at the mast to move the pole from one side to the other. The technique is only suitable for use on smaller yachts because the pole is allowed to float free during the gybe, which would not be safe with the long and heavy poles found on the bigger boats. Another limitation is that once the new guy is in the pole end, the pole has to be pushed out to the new windward side and this can end up as a bow and arrow affair, with the bowman pushing the point of the arrow against the force of the sail – not at all recommended if the loads are too great.

An end for end gybe can either be performed using single sheets on either side or with a double sheet and guy system. The latter is normally used on yachts at the larger end of the suitable range and in heavier winds. The chief advantage of using the double sheet and guy set up is that the spinnaker can be flown on the sheets during the gybe, allowing the pole to be gybed from and onto lazy guys. This obviously reduces the loads on the pole and makes the bowman's job that much easier and safer but it does involve two more pieces of rope and in light weather the extra weight on the clew of the spinnaker is unnecessary.

In general terms the manoeuvre will go as follows:-

1. 'Standby to Gybe' calls the skipper. At this the crew get into their positions. This is similar to the preparation for a dip pole gybe except that there will be no need for the topping lift to be lowered and the bowman need only go as far forward as the mast where he readies himself by getting the lazy guy in hand (if using double sheets and guys) and draping the windward genoa sheet over his shoulder so that it can be placed over the new outer pole end during the gybe. One of the cockpit crew eases a little slack into the downhaul to make it easier to push the pole out on the new windward side.

2. The helmsman gets ready for the gybe by ensuring that he is positioned so that he can steer effectively after the gybe. If on a yacht with tiller steering, this may well mean changing sides before the gybe so that he goes into it steering from leeward but comes out after the gybe steering from the new windward side.

3. As the helmsman bears away for the gybe, the pole is squared and the sheet eased. The spinnaker trimmer should have both sheets in hand and under tension so that he is controlling the sail throughout the gybe.

4. Once borne away to a run, the helmsman calls 'trip' or something similar and at this point the bowman takes the pole off the mast, puts the genoa sheet over the top of the pole end, clips the new guy (or sheet if using single ropes) into the jaws and pushes the pole out and forwards towards the clew of the sail. As the pole is pushed out on the new windward side, the bowman unclips the old guy and drops it away from the pole together with the other genoa sheet and then clips the pole back onto the mast – his task is now completed.

NB. When gybing in open water and clear of the constraints of other competitors, the helmsman can help the bowman considerably by steering the yacht slightly by the lee as the pole is taken off the mast. This will help to float the spinnaker away from the boat and relieve pressure on the pole. This can just be a matter of the bowman waiting a fraction of a second before taking the pole off the mast but the next stage is more crucial.

4

With the pole on the mast, the mainsail is gybed and the guy winched in to get the new spinnaker tack to the pole end. The old sheet is now released.

Fig 1.12 Spinnaker Gybe — End for End

NB: This system obviously requires a pole with special beaks at both ends. Both the pole topping lift and downhaul should be attached via bridles.

3

This can be the most difficult point of the gybe. The pole must be thrust both outward and forward and to achieve this the best position for the bowman is to stand braced with the back of his shoulder against the mast and be facing forward. It is also vital that the new guy is handled with sympathy from the cockpit; sufficient slack must be allowed so that the pole can be re-attached to the mast.

2

The guy is released and the kite is now controlled by the two sheets. The bowman unclips the pole from the mast and inserts the new guy into the beak and thrusts the pole across the boat and out to leeward, releasing the old guy from the other end of the pole.

1

The bowman has taken a bight of the new spinnaker guy forward to the mast. The lazy sheet is tensioned and put on a winch.

If the yacht is by the lee on the old gybe, the spinnaker will tend to be flying to windward and while this makes it easy to remove the pole from the mast, it also makes it next to impossible to push it out on the new side and re-attach the pole on the mast. It is therefore ideal if the helmsman can momentarily swing the yacht back towards the old gybe for just long enough to allow the bowman to get the pole clipped on again, he can then continue through the gybe as normal.

5. When the pole is clipped safely back on the mast, the bowman calls 'made', the new guy is tensioned (if using lazies) and the old sheet eased. At the same time the mainsail is gybed and the runners changed over as for a dip pole gybe.

Gybing with Asymmetric Spinnakers

As discussed later in the chapter on sail trim, asymmetric spinnakers can either be set on the centreline or at the end of a normal spinnaker pole. Because they are, by definition asymmetric, they cannot be gybed in the same way as a more normal symmetrical sail.

If the sail is set on the centreline, whether or not on a bowsprit, gybing is simplicity itself. The sail will be outside the forestay and the lazy sheet should be led around the front of the sail, dangling down on the stem fitting while not in use. As you set up for a gybe, the old sheet is allowed to run, the sail blows forward and flaps happily, then the new sheet is pulled in and the sail comes around to the new side.

The old sheet must be let go before bearing away beyond dead downwind otherwise the sail will blow inside the foretriangle and go the wrong side of the forestay. Also, the boat will be relatively slow while the sail is flapping so the new sheet needs to be brought in as quickly as possible, probably having one crew member sweating on the sheet direct from the sail to speed things up.

The mainsail is gybed just as at any other time.

If the asymmetric spinnaker is being flown from the end of a pole then life becomes somewhat more complicated. The simplest way to deal with the situation is to temporarily take the tack of the spinnaker down to the centreline using an adjustable tack strop, gybe the sail as above, then get the pole onto the new side, take the tack of the sail back to the pole end with the new guy and release the temporary tack strop and away you go.

To do this will entail having a guy on each side attached to the tack of the sail, a sheet either side attached to the clew with the lazy ropes going around the forestay and also a tack strop taken from the stem fitting or end of bowsprit to the tack in such a way that it can be tensioned during a gybe. The spinnaker pole should be used with the jaws opening downwards to allow the tack to be freed and pulled into the stem when required.

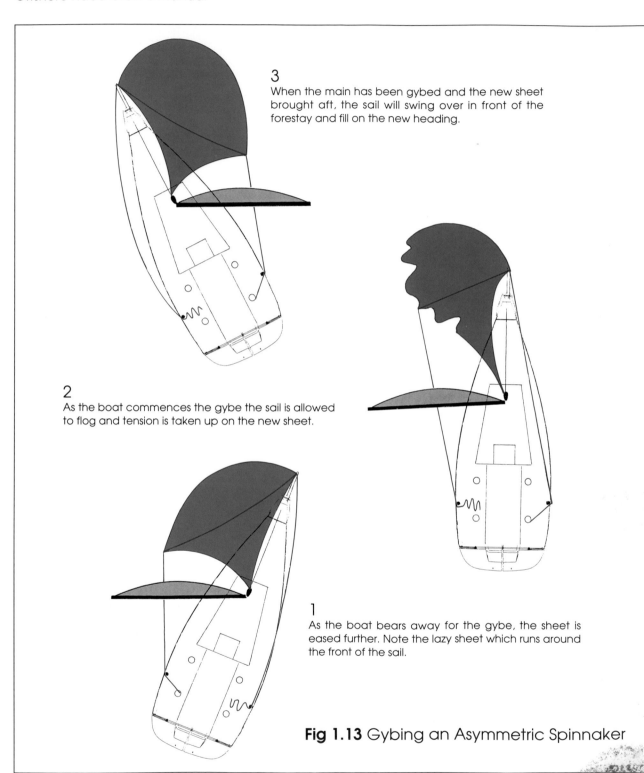

3
When the main has been gybed and the new sheet brought aft, the sail will swing over in front of the forestay and fill on the new heading.

2
As the boat commences the gybe the sail is allowed to flog and tension is taken up on the new sheet.

1
As the boat bears away for the gybe, the sheet is eased further. Note the lazy sheet which runs around the front of the sail.

Fig 1.13 Gybing an Asymmetric Spinnaker

Spinnaker Peeling

Spinnaker peeling is one of those manoeuvres that looks so slick when done properly, that many crews feel it is too ambitious for them to attempt. In reality it is one of the safer and simpler evolutions and merely relies on good preparation.

The principle is to attach the tack of the new sail to either the bow or the end of the pole, bend on a spare sheet and halyard, hoist the new sail, trip away the old sail from the guy, then attach the guy to the new sail, drop the old one and the job is complete.

The important points to bear in mind are as follows:-

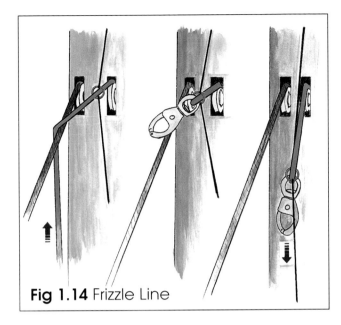

Fig 1.14 Frizzle Line

1. Whenever possible, the new sail should be hoisted on the halyard that is to windward at the masthead. This will allow you to set the new sail 'inside' the old one and to drop the old sail away to leeward without putting a twist into the halyards.

An inside peel using the leeward halyard is possible but will put a half twist in the halyards. This must then be removed by someone going up the mast, certainly before a second peel is performed and preferably before trying to drop the new spinnaker because the twist is likely to jam the halyards.

The system used on some racing yachts to obviate the need for someone to go to the masthead is 'frizzle lines'. These are lightweight, endless loops of line exiting the mast through small sheaves at the top and bottom. They have a metal ring attached to one point of the loop and this has the halyard running through it. This ring is usually left at the masthead so that it does not interfere with the normal operation of the halyard. If a twist in the halyards at the masthead occurs, the offending halyard can be hoisted to the top from the base of the mast and then pulled down, untwisted, by the frizzle line.

2. If the new sail is to go up inside the old one (which is to be preferred), the spare sheet needs to be rove inside the old one.

3. When using the windward halyard, it will have to be taken from the mast and around the forestay before being clipped onto the head of the new sail.

4. There are two ways to attach the tack of the new sail temporarily while the peel is happening.

a) A 1½ metre peeling strop can be tied or clipped onto the genoa tack fitting, with a half hitch around the forestay near its top. The tack of the sail is clipped to the end of this strop for hoisting. Once the new sail has been hoisted, the pole is eased inboard until the bowman can reach the guy to trip the old sail away. Once this has been done, the guy is let fly completely and pulled down and clipped onto the new sail. Then the guy is retensioned and as the load comes off the peeling strop it is tripped away to allow the guy to move up and aft.

The strop is attached to the tack of the blue spinnaker.

Fig 1.15 Peeling Strop

Photo 1.21 A peeling shackle clipped to the bowman's harness.

b) The second method is somewhat neater but is only really suitable for use either on a close reach or on larger yachts (say over 12 metres). Here a peeling shackle is used. This is simply two snap-shackles attached back to back, either welded directly together or attached with a shackle.

The peeling shackle is attached to the pole, normally to the topping lift fitting and is then clipped onto the old sail. The guy is then tripped from the old sail while leaving it through the jaws of the pole. This leaves the sail unaffected except for a slight jerk as the old guy is tripped off. The guy is then clipped onto the tack of the new sail which is then hoisted. Once the new sail is up and set, the old sail is tripped away from the peeling shackle and dropped and the peeling shackle is removed from the pole.

On smaller yachts this technique can only be used when you are sailing on a close reach and the end of the pole is within reach from the deck (or by standing on the pulpit). On larger yachts the bowman would normally climb out along the downhaul to the end of the pole, taking the tack of the new spinnaker with him and do the work while sitting on top of the pole. One area of potential danger in this situation, is if the new sail is hoisted before it is clipped to the guy – the bowman will usually have it clipped temporarily to his harness and it is entirely possible for him to be flipped off the pole by a flogging spinnaker. In my experience, the crew doing the hoisting would only ever make that mistake once because the average bowman is not slow to let his feelings about such a thing known!

5. Once the new sail is fully hoisted it should be sheeted in and set as normal. The old sail will fly out to leeward, doing very little harm once it has been tripped away from the guy and it can be dropped and pulled into the cockpit in relatively leisurely fashion.

Photo 1.22 The bowman hauls the tack of the new spinnaker to the end of the pole during a peel.

6. Finally, once the old sail is inboard, the proper sheet and lazy guy can be clipped onto the new sail and the temporary sheet removed.

Spinnaker Drops – General Points

Whenever the spinnaker is being dropped, there are a few basic points that should be borne in mind. The drop needs to be safe – that is, there should be little or no chance of things getting out of hand and the spinnaker ending up in the water. The crew involved in the manoeuvre need to understand the loads that will suddenly be imposed on different control lines as the drop proceeds so as to be ready to deal with them. The spinnaker should be brought down in such a way that whatever else is going on in the yacht simultaneously can still proceed with reasonable efficiency. As with any other sail change, the key to success is in planning and preparation.

There are many ways of achieving a spinnaker drop and we look at some of these in the following paragraphs. Before getting into specifics there are some techniques general to most drops:-

1. The halyard must be ready to run. This means that it should have been flaked (not coiled) at some stage before the drop commences. If the tail of the halyard 'lives' on it's own winch, it can be flaked into figure of eights before being stored on the winch and when needed the whole tail can be lifted off the winch, turned over and laid on the deck ready for the drop. If, on the other hand, the tail 'lives' down the main hatch, it should be pulled out just before the drop and fed back down again to ensure it has not got tangled with other ropes or hooked around some piece of cabin furniture.

2. Although it is generally best to let the halyard run unimpeded, there are often times when it will be necessary to stop the spinnaker from dropping too fast or too far. For this reason, the halyard must always be led either around a winch (which can be used for snubbing it) or through a clutch. Trying to stop a spinnaker from dragging in the water with your bare hands is not usually very successful!

3. Once the sail is down, tidying up can usually be left for at least a few moments and it is normally best to get the crew and yacht settled again before worrying about things like re-reeving sheets etc. The exception to this is obviously the tidying up that is necessary to perform the next manoeuvre, especially if that is to follow immediately after the drop. An example of this will be to get the spinnaker pole lowered and to ensure the genoa sheets are led over it correctly if you need to tack shortly after the drop.

4. Before dropping the spinnaker, the genoa should be hoisted and the mainsail set for the next leg. If you have been running under spinnaker it is probable that the genoa halyard will have been used to pull the rig forward and since it will be under tension and helping to support the mast, it will need to be released with some care. Also, when the halyard is released, the runners should be tensioned sufficiently to stop the forestay flopping around. Mainsail controls need to be adjusted ready for the next leg and it is usually better to get this done before the last minute and therefore before the spinnaker is dropped.

Spinnaker Drop – Simple Guy Run

In most situations the easiest and most reliable method to drop a spinnaker is to let the guy run and then pull the sail in to leeward using either the sheet or preferably the lazy guy. This method has some pitfalls which may not be obvious until you have seen them yourself, but if care is taken to avoid these, it nearly always gives a safe drop.

1. Genoa is hoisted, mainsail is prepared for the next leg as usual.

2. The lazy sheet (if using double sheets and guys) and the working guy must be made free to run and the halyard is also prepared for the drop.

3. One or more crew get hold of the lazy guy ready to pull the sail into the yacht. The position that the sail is pulled in will vary according to the configuration of the yacht, the point of sailing at the time and the wind strength, but as a general fall-back position, it can always be pulled straight into the main hatch, under the boom.(See Photos 1.24, 1.25, 1.26 & 1.27 and Fig 1.17)

4. The guy and the halyard should be released simultaneously – this collapses the spinnaker. Once the pole has gone forward to the forestay, the guy should be checked until the spinnaker is halfway into the boat and totally under control.

Photo 1.23 The headsail is hoisted prior to dropping the spinnaker.

Photo 1.24 The guy and the spinnaker halyard have been released. It is vital that these two lines plus the lazy sheet have been prepared to run unimpeded. The pole has started its descent to the deck and the bowman attends the forward end of the pole to free the guy and be ready to stow it once the mast end has been lowered. The pitman will control the final few feet of the halyard drop to make sure that the kite does not fall into the sea. Spare crew are working frantically to pull the spinnaker directly into the main hatch and below so that the boat will be clear for the next leg and to tack if necessary.

Photo 1.25 A busy time for all the crew! As the spinnaker is fully tamed and sent below, the cockpit team are busy clearing winches and also the immediate debris of redundant sheets, guys and the like, so that the boat can manoeuvre freely on the next leg. One mistake is however quite obvious in that the headsail sheet has been cleated and is left unattended – the power from that sail may prove vital in gaining places at the mark and to keep boat speed to its maximum.

Photo 1.26 As the boat hardens up to come onto a beat the last remnants of the spinnaker vanish down the main hatch. Both the headsail and the mainsail trimmers are sheeting in hard and the bowman secures the pole down on deck, making sure that the headsail sheets are clear to tack and that the topping lift is moved aft to the mast. The rest of the crew are hiking out hard on the windward side-deck pretending to be double their weight.

Photo 1.27 The bowman's legs are visible below the boom as he sprints back from the foredeck to his windward side-deck station. The trimmers are working at obtaining optimum speed and the pitman will be clipping the sheets and guys together so that they can be moved at will from the deck. The important thing is to keep the boat on her feet and making best speed and direction as soon as she comes on the wind. The final tidying of lines and spinnaker repacking take second place – unless it's an extremely short beat to the next hoist.

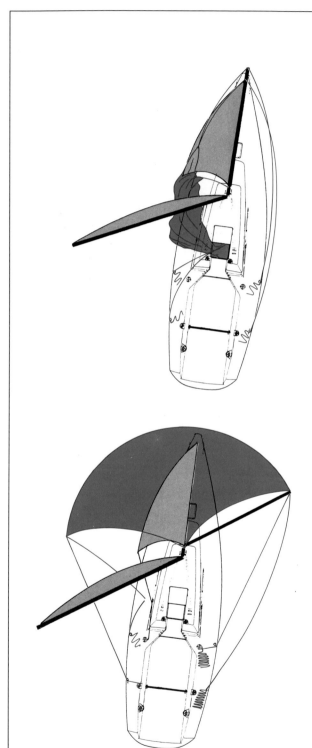

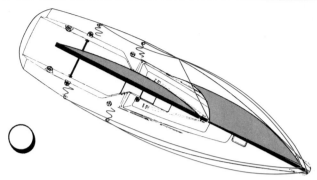

3

As soon as the boat hardens up, the vital thing is for the crew to balance the boat, and in anything other than light airs this usually means getting out on the weather rail at the expense of all else. The single crew below can clip both sets of sheets and guys together along with the halyard. All that then needs to be done is to secure these lines by tensioning them from the cockpit and cleating them off. General tidying up can be left until the helmsman and trimmers have brought the boat up to optimum windward performance.

2

On the drop, the guy is released at the same moment as the spinnaker halyard and the sail will be pulled quickly into the bowels of the boat via the companionway. (Both the guy trimmer and halyard man should keep an eye on the sail so that they can check its descent if it looks as though the kite will hit the water before the retrieving crew can get it aboard — spinnaker trawling is slow!)

The headsail is trimmed to keep all available power on as the boat approaches and then rounds the mark. The topping lift is lowered so the bowman can ready the boat for a quick tack, if called, when the boat comes on the wind.

1

The headsail has been hoisted and is left under-trimmed so that it does not interfere with the air flow around the spinnaker. The working guy is still around its winch, but the tail has been flaked ready to run free on the drop. The lazy spinnaker sheet is also flaked as it must also be free to run around the forestay when the guy is released. The lazy guy on the leeward beam will be used to pull the descending kite into the boat.

Fig 1.17 Leeward Spinnaker Drop

Spinnaker Drop – Float Drop

When approaching a leeward mark and you need to gybe at the mark, there are two options open. The first and simplest is simply to drop the spinnaker a little early, get rid of the pole and then gybe around the buoy with the genoa and mainsail. In windy weather or if approaching the mark on a reach or downwind with the current under you, this will always be the preferred option.

Whenever coming to the leeward mark on a run in light winds, especially against the current, it will be important to keep the spinnaker set for as long as possible. As soon as the sail is dropped, your speed will decrease dramatically and ground (and possibly places) will be lost. In these situations, it is preferable to keep the spinnaker drawing right up to the mark, but obviously the pole must be cleared before you gybe the genoa otherwise all sorts of chaos will ensue and this is where the float drop provides a solution.

As you approach the mark, set the mainsail controls for upwind and hoist the genoa as normal. Then take the load on both spinnaker sheets and when the boat is more or less on a run, trip the pole away from the guy and lower it into the centre of the foredeck. The spinnaker should be kept drawing by trimming both sheets while this is happening and continued to be so right up to the buoy. Once the yacht reaches the buoy and you start to turn for the gybe, the spinnaker can be dropped, normally down the fore hatch since this will keep the cockpit clear for the genoa trimmers.

The sail can either be lowered on the old leeward side or the old windward side, the choice depending mainly on the exact wind angle as the mark is approached. When broad reaching in to the mark, the old leeward side is easiest but if it is a dead square run for the last couple of boat lengths, then it will be simplest to drop to leeward *after* the gybe has commenced. The reason for this is to prevent the sail falling in the water and under the bow as it is dropped. When coming in on a broad reach, most of the sail will be to leeward as you approach the mark and it can simply be dropped without a problem. If on the other hand you are dead square, then at least half of the sail will be to windward and as you start to turn the rest of the sail will blow onto the old windward side, thus making it much safer to drop late and on the new leeward side.

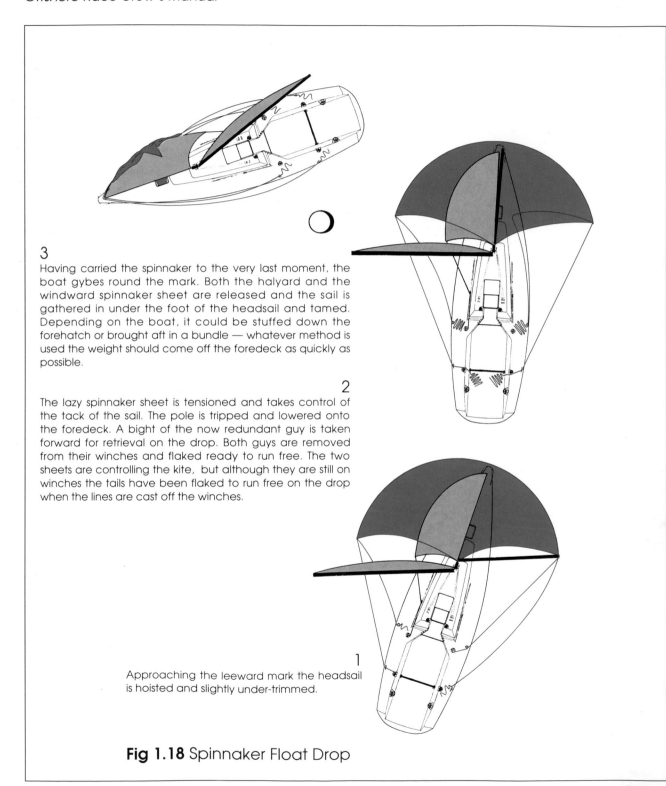

3

Having carried the spinnaker to the very last moment, the boat gybes round the mark. Both the halyard and the windward spinnaker sheet are released and the sail is gathered in under the foot of the headsail and tamed. Depending on the boat, it could be stuffed down the forehatch or brought aft in a bundle — whatever method is used the weight should come off the foredeck as quickly as possible.

2

The lazy spinnaker sheet is tensioned and takes control of the tack of the sail. The pole is tripped and lowered onto the foredeck. A bight of the now redundant guy is taken forward for retrieval on the drop. Both guys are removed from their winches and flaked ready to run free. The two sheets are controlling the kite, but although they are still on winches the tails have been flaked to run free on the drop when the lines are cast off the winches.

1

Approaching the leeward mark the headsail is hoisted and slightly under-trimmed.

Fig 1.18 Spinnaker Float Drop

Chapter 2

Crew Work By Position Within The Boat

This chapter looks at each individual crew member and at the roles and tasks which are usually defined as coming within that area of responsibility. A certain amount of time is spent considering the attributes necessary to enable a crew to be good at his or her particular position aboard and a large part of each section deals with the jobs themselves.

The previous chapter on crew work by manoeuvre looked at the same subject from a slightly different viewpoint and the chapter on sail trim will deal with that subject in more depth than is covered here. As with most aspects of sailing and racing, there are many ways to achieve the same object and these notes are only intended as a guide. If you do not fit exactly into my idea of the perfect bowman/trimmer/pitman or whatever, but still feel that you are in the best slot within the crew for your talent, then do not worry overmuch. Even on yachts racing at the highest international levels, many crew look unlikely candidates for their positions on the boat!

The Bowman

The good bowman has a number of physical and mental features that are fairly easily identifiable. One of the first points to make is that although this section is entitled the 'bowMAN', the job can be done just as well by women. On larger yachts, it is true that a fair amount of brute strength is required and in these cases the job would not be an obvious choice for the average woman. However, on smaller yachts, say up to about ten metres overall length, there is no need for this role to be thought of as one needing huge amounts of strength.

The main physical characteristics that will always be required are good balance, a head for heights and reasonable upper body strength. In some cases it can help to be tall, although this is by no means essential, but it is important to have a good power to weight ratio and to be able to lift one's own body – as when practising chin-ups in the gym – otherwise it will not be feasible to climb to the end of the spinnaker pole without assistance (needed on larger yachts) or to clamber up the mast with a halyard acting simply as a safety line. Actual weight is not very critical and will need to be balanced against strength and speed. Although most yachts lose speed while they have someone working on the foredeck, it is often better to have a heavy person there for a short time than for a lighter person to spend twice as long doing the same job.

Mentally the job can be quite demanding. There are numerous occasions when a bowman must work on his own with virtually no communication with the back-end of the boat. Often the role is highly visible from both on and off the yacht and having an extrovert personality can help. The person who wishes to do a good job as a member of the team whilst remaining innocuously in amongst the rest of the crew is unlikely to revel in this role. This is not to say that a bowman is set apart from the rest of the team, far from it. He must be prepared to work with the others or they can make his task next to impossible. Apart from all the other concerns the job brings, it is very easy to be made into the fall-guy by the helmsman – when he messes up a gybe it is the bowman who is likely to be shouted at for not being quick enough! There are two ways of dealing with this situation, preferably ignore the comments at the time and get on with the job – but discuss it with the helmsman later, or allow yourself to become rattled and then really make some mistakes.

Being at the sharp end puts the bowman into

the coldest, wettest and potentially the most dangerous part of the yacht, so a degree of fearlessness is required, although this must not be allowed to degenerate into recklessness. A good head for heights is pretty well essential since there will inevitably be times when the job will entail going up the mast. Seasickness can be a real problem when working at the extreme end of the boat. There is always maximum movement here, and changing a headsail while slamming into a big sea is a bit like riding a roller coaster – people with strong stomachs are the ones most likely to enjoy the job.

Equipment Required by the Bowman

It is pretty obvious that the bow is going to be one of the wettest places onboard and this necessitates the bowman having different clothing from, say the navigator or helmsman who sit in relative shelter at the aft end.

Most bowman find that a dry suit, or at least a smock with latex neck and cuff seals, is almost essential, especially for round-the-cans racing where ease of movement is very important. Offshore, if a dry suit is worn it must be remembered that they are not usually warm in themselves and good quality underwear and middle layer clothes will be necessary to stop you getting really cold in the long spells between short bursts of frantic activity.

Good, really non-slip footwear is also important and windsurfer bootees with ultra soft rubber soles are to be seen on a number of boats, as are the type of dinghy boots which lace up tightly at the side. Classic, loose fitting sailing boots tend to be too heavy and cumbersome. Sailing shoes are OK in warm climates but not offshore in the early season of the higher latitudes.

On boats over about eleven metres there will be many occasions when it is necessary to go either to the masthead or to the outer end of the spinnaker pole. A climbing harness will be

Photo 2.1 The bowman has the wettest job on the boat and therefore good robust waterproof clothing is vital. This set of skins has high-waisted trousers with Velcro tabs around the ankles. The top has a high storm-proof collar and hood and the front opening is secured with a heavy zip with flap-over protection. The cuffs are also storm proofed with Velcro tabs.
The harness worn is suitable for climbing the mast or to reach the end of the spinnaker pole for a gybe. Strengthened knees are important since the bowman spends much time scrabbling around the deck on all fours. (Usually ashore as well!)

needed for those acrobatics. This should normally be part of the bowman's own equipment since it must fit really well and be comfortable. A normal cruising bosun's chair is not at all suitable since it does not allow the wearer to climb or allow him sufficient agility and it is only really intended for someone to be winched aloft. Most bowman use a screwgate karabiner for their attachment to a halyard, preferring these to either reliance on an ordinary snap shackle or to the inconvenience of a screw type shackle. Climbing shops sell very light aluminium karabiners which are ideal for the purpose along with the harnesses themselves. If the harness is well adjusted and can be put on at a moment's notice, then it may be more comfortable to have it handy on longer races, only putting it on when needed.

Another essential for use when peeling spinnakers is a set of back to back snap shackles. These allow the new sail to be attached at the tack without hassle. A sharp knife allows you to cut a rope if absolutely essential (for example if you get tangled in a working rope). While I would rarely suggest that the bowman should be doing the navigation, there are numerous occasions when a hand bearing compass would come in handy and obviously a watch with a count-down facility is a must for timing the start sequence.

Safety is the final point to consider. When sailing offshore and particularly at night, the possibility of the bowman falling over the side needs to be taken seriously. The absolute minimum is a whistle and small personal torch. If the torch has a powerful enough beam to see as far as the hounds to check halyards for twist, then so much the better. A personal strobe light or even a personal EPIRB can also be useful in really rough conditions.

Where separate sheets and guys are being used or if spinnaker peeling is on the menu of options, a fid or spike for tripping the old spinnaker clear is another essential. There are different shapes of these according to the make of snapshackle in use, so it is sensible for this to be part of the yacht's equipment. When working on the bow I like to have the fid attached to my harness by a length of thin shock-cord so it is always with me when needed – a second, spare fid stowed with the boat's knife and pliers is also a good idea.

Bowman – Training

The bowman's job on a racing yacht requires a reasonably high level of personal fitness as well as strong arms and fingers – and even more importantly, good mobility and balance. Any physical training programme should relate to these requirements, since it is all too easy to overdevelop some muscle groups to an extent that would hinder parts of the bowman's task. An example would be if a training programme was followed that concentrated on weights and leg development. This may not do much for overall stamina and could leave you less flexible and slower than before.

Aerobics, swimming and similar exercises are always good for overall fitness, while some work with chin-ups, press-ups and a certain amount of weight-lifting can be used to develop the arms and shoulders. Flexibility and balance can be enhanced by participating in certain sports such as five-a-side football, tennis or judo.

Bowman – Boat Preparation

I am a great believer in each crew member spending some time ensuring that his or her part of the boat is as well set up as possible. For the bowman this will include such things as taping any open fairleads to prevent ropes becoming caught, making sure that all the spinnaker pole gear works properly, getting the topping lift marked for gybes and so on.

The Bowman's Role at the Start

At the start of a race the bowman must not only get the required headsail ready to hoist, but must also be able to give good, accurate information to the tactician and to the helmsman with regard to the line and to overlap situations.

Headsail preparation is somewhat simplified at the start because the most likely sail will be tried in the pre-start period and then dropped again until about five or six minutes before the preparatory signal. Unless the weather conditions are very stable, it is usually sensible to repack this sail while leaving the tack and clew clipped on. This means that the sail can easily be replaced in the event of a sudden wind change. The bowman must liaise with the afterguard as to when the headsail is to be hoisted and at what stage they are no longer 'allowed' to change their minds on headsail selection. Remember that on a windy day it usually takes a little longer to hoist and set a sail than on a day with little wind.

During the final run in to the starting line it is vital that the bowman has a feel for the exact position of the boat relative to the line. To achieve this he must obtain transits along the line before the start. When calling the distance from the line it is normal to give the perpendicular distance rather than to try to judge the distance to sail on a particular course. This leaves it up to the tactician to estimate actual time to run and so on. It is often not possible to shout distances back from the bow to the tactician and therefore a good visual communication system is required between the bowman and the back end. The most commonly used system is for the bowman to hold up fingers to indicate boat lengths from the line. A clenched fist means 'on the line' and a downward motion with the hand tells the tactician that you are over the line and need to duck back before you can start properly.

Similar sign language needs to be used to

Photo 2.2 Prior to the 10 minute gun, a trial beat will have resulted in the choice of sail that is inserted into the luff groove and is ready to hoist. If the wind is unsteady, there may well be a change of mind – hence a second sail still on deck.

indicate overlap situations. It is only in marginal overlaps that the tactician will need help and the normal reason for his concern is to determine whether it is possible to bear away or luff behind a transom. The normal signs to use are thumbs up to mean that there is NO overlap and you are therefore free to

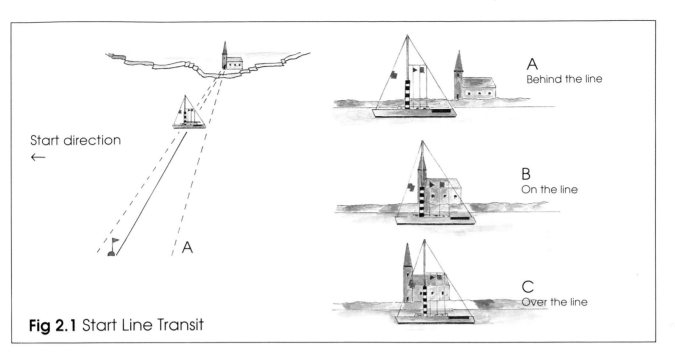

Fig 2.1 Start Line Transit

Start direction
←

A
Behind the line

B
On the line

C
Over the line

alter course as you like and thumbs down to indicate that an overlap exists.

The bowman must understand the racing rules at least so far as they affect him and he will need to have read the relevant parts of the sailing instructions so that he knows the definition of the start line.

The Bowman's Role During a Tack

During an ordinary tack the bowman does not have a great deal to do. His main function will be to ensure that neither the sheets nor the clew of the headsail get snagged during the tack and then to 'skirt' the foot of the sail inside the guard-rails if necessary.

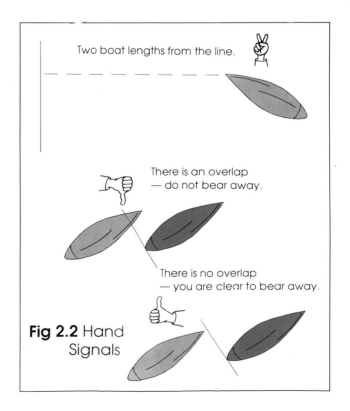

Two boat lengths from the line.

There is an overlap
— do not bear away.

There is no overlap
— you are clear to bear away.

Fig 2.2 Hand Signals

Photo 2.3 One of the bowman's roles during any headsail hoist is to check that the sail runs freely through the pre-feeder and up the luff groove. On some systems the first two or three feet of the headfoil can become worn and tend to allow the sail to pull out backwards when commencing the hoist. The only answer to this problem is a new headfoil.

Bowman – Headsail Changing

Headsail changing can be one of those times when the bowman is glad to have done some work-outs in the gym. It can be physically tough, especially in rough weather.

A tack change should be fairly straightforward. While one of the other crew fetches the sail, the bowman prepares the halyard, looking up to make sure there are no twists in the system. The halyard is clipped onto the head of the sail which is then dragged to the bow along the windward side. The tack is clipped on and the head fed through the pre-feeder and into the luff groove. As soon as this is done the sail should be ready for hoisting since another crewman should have already bent on the lazy sheet and adjusted the fairlead position.

If the bag has been set up properly it should

be able to burst open as the sail is hoisted, otherwise the zipper will need to be opened first. If you do not have break-away bags, it may be worth the bowman taking the sail out of the bag before he goes to the bow, dragging the sail along the deck by the sail-tie around the luff. In any case be careful not to lose the bag! Depending on the yacht, the bowman may go back to the mast to sweat up the halyard or he may stay at the bow and help feed the sail into the groove.

Once the sail is virtually at the top, the boat is tacked and the old sail dropped. The bowman's job is to get the old sail down and off the bow as quickly as possible. The old halyard can be passed directly to the mastman for stowing and the sail dragged back and either repacked on the side-deck or bundled below for packing later.

When an inside set/outside drop straight line genoa change is called for, the same set will be used except that the trimmer will need to bend on and lead a new sheet on the working side. However, once the new sail has been hoisted the bowman will really notice the difference. He must get the old sail down on the outside of the new one and this is obviously much harder than dropping it on the windward side. He will need to sit right forward in the pulpit and reach around the forestay to pull down a metre or so of the luff tape, then unclip the tack of the old sail before dragging the sail under the foot of the genoa to prevent it falling in the water. On larger yachts this will almost certainly be a job for at least two people or the sail will end up in the sea.

For a straight line outside set, a somewhat different initial procedure is followed. Here, the bowman should be preparing the halyard and taking it to the bow, around the back and outside of the old sail, while someone else gets the new sail. If using a wire halyard, his job will be made easier by tying a sail-tie to the snapshackle as this will bend around the foot of the old sail much more readily.

Once at the bow, the halyard can be temporally attached to the rail while the head of the new sail is fed under the foot of the old one and then into the pre-feeder and leeward luff groove. To attach the tack of the new sail at this stage will only make life harder and this should be left until the sail is almost completely hoisted. The bowman should sit right forward as the new sail is going up, pulling the luff under the old sail and as far forward as possible to prevent it pulling back and ripping out of the luff groove. Taking the old sail down once the new genoa is up and set is the same as for a tack change.

Bowman – Spinnaker Hoists

The greater part of the bowman's job during this manoeuvre will be done long before the hoist itself. Here, good fast preparation is the surest route to a successful hoist. Assume that the boat is beating up to the windward mark and most of the preparation can be performed on the windward side and timed to coincide with the last few tacks. The bowman should liaise with the tactician to ensure that when his weight is off the rail it is doing as little harm as possible to boat speed. At some point, however, he must decide that if he leaves it any later the hoist will be jeopardised and be prepared to say this.

When two spinnaker halyards are available it is usually best to use the leeward one. This will allow one inside spinnaker peel at a later stage without creating a twist in the halyards at the masthead. (The only time that this is not true is when the boat will be gybed before a peel is necessary, in which case it is obviously better to use the windward halyard.) Whichever is to be used must be taken forward so that it is outside the genoa (and genoa sheets), is the correct side of the forestay and is not wrapped around any other ropes (such as the pole topping lift). It is often best to flick the bight of the halyard behind the spreaders to keep it clear of the genoa, especially if one or more tacks are to be made before the hoist.

3

When the boat tacks back onto starboard on its final run in to the mark, the spinnaker halyard is clipped to the kite and the pole raised to its correct position. The guy is also put on its winch. As the boat rounds the mark all will be prepared for an instant hoist.

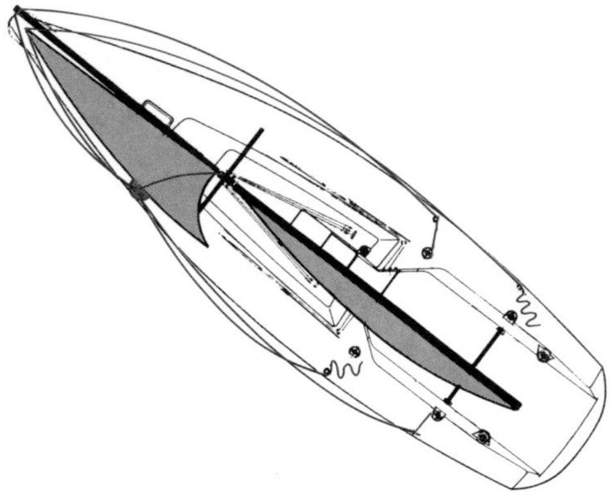

2

When the boat tacks onto port on its final approach to the windward mark, the bowman should secure the spinnaker turtle to the weather rail and connect the sheets and guys. The sheet should be put on a winch and the lazy guy cleared to run freely.

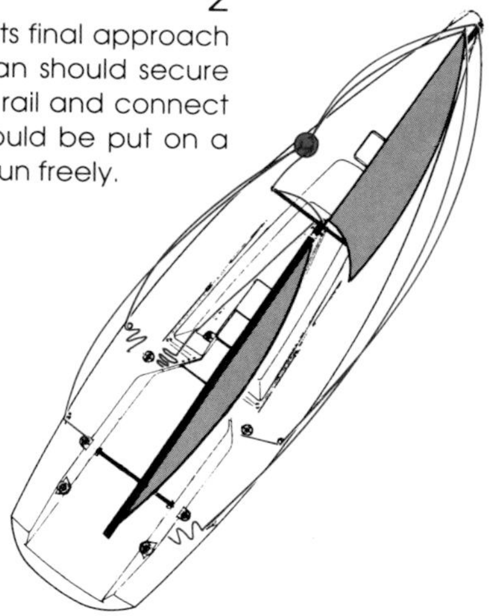

1

Both sets of sheets and guys are secured in the correct position for a starboard tack bear-away set. (Position X) The guy can be clipped into the pole beak.

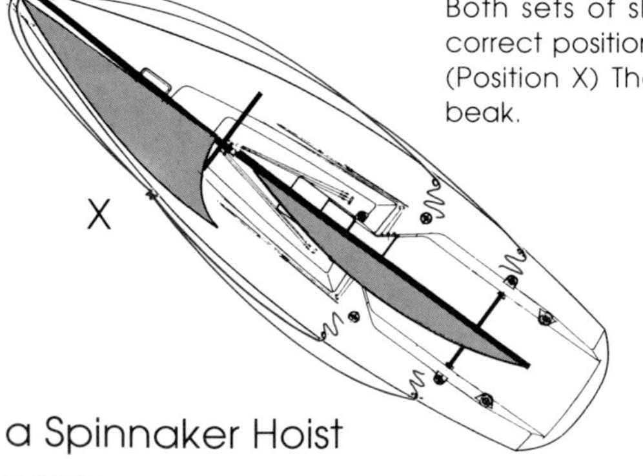

X

Fig 2.3 Setting Up for a Spinnaker Hoist

The sheets and guys (if lazies are being used) must clipped on to the spinnaker, ensuring that they are all outside the forestay and shrouds and that they have not accidentally become rove through the guard-rails or under headsail sheets. When setting up on leaving the dock or after a spinnaker drop, I like to clip the sheets and guys together leaving one sheet snap shackle free and open, ready to be clipped to the sail. There is no need to clip them to the rail because when they are left free it is easy for the cockpit crew to pull the shackles to the required side without the need for anyone to go forward.

On an ordinary bear away set on a windy and rough day, it is sometimes worth setting the spinnaker bag up on the windward side, halfway along the foredeck. The ends of the sheets, guys and halyard can all be brought under the foot of the genoa and up the spinnaker on the windward side from where it should hoist with no problem. This prevents the spinnaker being washed overboard, especially if you are going to be on the same tack for a lengthy period on your way in to the mark.(See Fig 1.8)

The inboard end of the pole can be set up on the mast, the downhaul and topping lift checked and the guy inserted in the pole end. Once this basic preparation has been completed, the bowman should get off the foredeck and back on the rail as soon as possible. The final task of helping the pole up to the horizontal can be left until the final few seconds before the hoist. Once sitting back on the rail, it is always worth the bowman looking around to check carefully that there are no twists or other mistakes.

When performing a gybe set, the spinnaker bag should be positioned as near to the bow as possible and even put in the pulpit if it is small enough. This keeps it forward of the genoa during the gybe and helps to prevent snarl-ups. Otherwise the job of the bowman is virtually the same as for a simple bear away set. The only other point that may be worth considering, especially if the topping lift exits from very high up on the mast, is to take the topping lift around the leech of the genoa and under the genoa foot before clipping it onto the pole. This will allow the pole to be topped a fraction earlier because the genoa sheet will be inside the topping lift and will therefore not need to be completely slack before the pole can be topped.

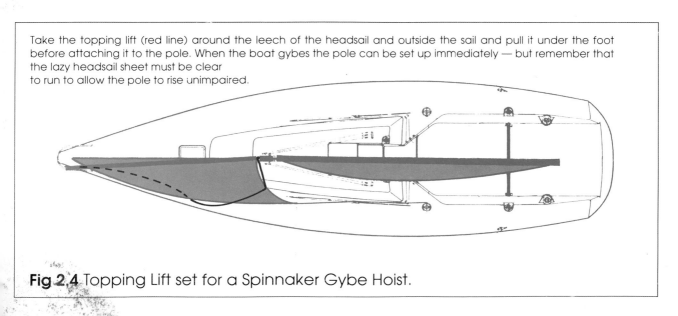

Take the topping lift (red line) around the leech of the headsail and outside the sail and pull it under the foot before attaching it to the pole. When the boat gybes the pole can be set up immediately — but remember that the lazy headsail sheet must be clear
to run to allow the pole to rise unimpaired.

Fig 2.4 Topping Lift set for a Spinnaker Gybe Hoist.

In any hoist, the priority will be to get the spinnaker up and setting really fast. In all but the windiest weather this will mean getting the genoa down at least partway as soon as the spinnaker hits the top. The bowman must be ready to pull the genoa down and prevent it falling in the water. As usual, he should pull it down quickly and then either put a quick sail-tie around it and leave it forward or else drag it off the foredeck ready for packing. If the mast is fitted with in-line spreaders and it is normal to wind the rig forward while running, the bowman should take the genoa halyard off the sail and clip it onto the tack fitting.

Bowman – Spinnaker Gybing

A gybe exposes the bowman to more potential hazard than any other task and often leaves him as the scapegoat to cover for the inadequacies of the helmsman!

In a dip pole gybe there is really very little for the bowman to do. He will need to be right forward as the pole comes in and down to him, with a bight of the lazy guy in his hands ready to put into the jaws of the pole. Either he can trip the pole open himself by using a long tripping line or the mastman can do it for him. As he puts the new guy in the pole and closes the jaws he should shout 'made' very loudly to let the cockpit crew know he has done his job.

The two most common errors in a dip pole gybe are for the lazy guy to be put into the jaws backwards, which results in a twist as it comes under load, or secondly and even more frequently, when the bowman lets go of the pole too early and when there is still considerable slack in the new guy. Then a loop of this slack can fall under the pole and jam under load. The former problem is one which can be cured by practising but the latter is about timing. Once the guy is in the end of the pole and 'made' has been called, the bowman should hold the pole for the second or two that it takes until the guy comes taught and the pole is pulled from his hand.

When reach to reach gybing, the clew of the spinnaker will be a long way aft as the boat approaches the gybe and as the sail is squared there will be a vast amount of slack in the new guy which exacerbates the above problem and makes it even harder for the cockpit crew on the new guy. In this situation, the bowman should stand at the mast with his bight of the lazy guy in hand and only go forward with it as the clew starts to go forward. In this way there should be just the right amount of slack to make the gybe easy once the spinnaker is fully squared.

End for end gybes on smaller yachts have the bowman actually working at the mast, with or without a second person depending on the wind strength. Here he must take the pole off the mast, clip the other end of the pole onto the new guy and then push the pole out and forward before finally clipping the new end of the pole back onto the mast.

He must be positioned securely so that he is not trying to use the pole to balance himself – it should be him controlling the pole! It will always be necessary to push the pole forwards at the same time as outwards and his position should reflect this need. The most acceptable stance at the outset is to face forward and slightly to windward with the back of the shoulder braced against the front of the mast. In the ideal situation, the windward genoa sheet should always be over the end of the pole and this will necessitate dropping off the old sheet as the pole comes in and placing the new sheet over the pole end before clipping in the guy and pushing it out. Although this is ideal, the bowman should remember that it can be done later and it is more important to get the pole back on the mast quickly.

Bowman – Peeling Spinnakers

The full procedures for peeling spinnakers have been dealt with in chapter one on crewwork by manoeuvre. Suffice to say here that peeling is all about preparation, mainly by the bowman. It is also worth noting that on larger yachts, the bowman will need to go to the end of the pole with the tack of the new sail and should practise this in clement weather inshore before attempting it offshore at night. It is nearly always safer and easier for the bowman to go to the pole end with a halyard attached to his harness and in all but the lightest of conditions he should be persuaded of this fact – it is very slow to drop two spinnakers at once and then turn round to pick up a macho bowman from the water!

Bowman – Spinnaker Drops

When the time comes to dump the spinnaker there will be another few minutes of hectic activity for the bowman. In an ideal world he would have anticipated this and prepared as much as possible beforehand.

Unless the genoa halyard is clipped to the tack-fitting, it may need to be taken over the pole before it can be used. Assuming the genoa sheet is already over the pole, a bight of this can be attached to the halyard aft of the pole and then pulled around, bringing the halyard with it. The correct genoa needs to be on the foredeck and it is always prudent for the bowman to ask if any change is required before

bending the sail on – sometimes the run will have been so busy for the skipper/tactician that he has not had time to notice a rising or falling wind. Except on very small yachts, I believe it is nearly always worth packing the genoa immediately after it has been dropped and to leave the bag on deck. This makes a last minute change considerably easier for all concerned. If the genoa is still clipped on at the luff and the yacht is on the opposite gybe from when it was dropped, it will need to be taken to the new leeward side. It should be taken forward of the pole downhaul, untying the sheets if necessary.

At the spinnaker drop itself, the bowman helps the genoa up as required and then must be ready to down the pole quickly if a tack is imminent. One useful rule for everyone to remember, is not to tack after a spinnaker drop until the bowman has made a positive statement to the effect that the boat is 'clear to tack'. If there is no requirement to tack quickly, apart from helping the outer end of the pole into the centre of the foredeck, any other clearing up can be left until target boat speed has been achieved.

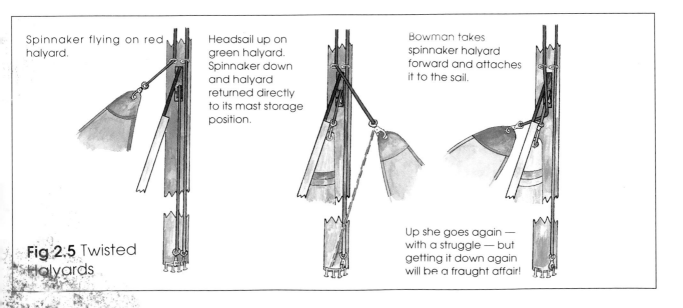

Spinnaker flying on red halyard.

Headsail up on green halyard. Spinnaker down and halyard returned directly to its mast storage position.

Bowman takes spinnaker halyard forward and attaches it to the sail.

Fig 2.5 Twisted Halyards

Up she goes again — with a struggle — but getting it down again will be a fraught affair!

Mast and Pit.

So far in this chapter we have looked at the role and position of the bowman. This is a fairly easily defined role and one which is necessary on virtually all offshore racing boats. The situation when dealing with the mast/halyards/pit area is somewhat more complicated. Here, the deck layout and size of yacht will determine exactly what jobs need covering and how many crew it will take to do them all. To demonstrate what I mean, it is worth looking at three examples; one on a small yacht, one on a well planned racing yacht and the final one from a cruiser-racer where simplicity for cruising may outweigh racing ergonomics.

In the case of the small racing yacht, say something like a J24, the bowman will also do most of the work at the mast (except sometimes!). There will be one middle of the boat crewman who does all the tasks within the pit area. In a spinnaker take-down the pitman will be quite capable of both controlling the halyard and also retrieving the spinnaker and it will only be on rare, windy occasions that the bowman will need any help at the mast.

Moving on to the middle sized, flat-out racing boat, here we will normally end up with a separate bowman and mastman, although often the mastman is effectively only the bowman's back-up, but once again it is likely that all halyards and similar controls will be led back to the pit area and will be within reach of one person. In anything other than really windy weather, the pitman will still be able to release and gather spinnakers on his own and in most situations he will be able to cope with all the controls.

It is when one attempts to exercise racing manoeuvres on a boat which is really designed for cruising that the jobs seem to expand to fill more and more crew numbers. I have raced extensively on a Swan 53 and here, not only is the yacht large enough to need both bowman and mastman, but it also requires a second person on the bow as an assistant. There is no pit as such and the halyard winches and other controls, such as spinnaker pole up and downhauls are positioned around the deck so that it all looks very efficient in that there is a different winch for each purpose. However, the fact is that no two ropes can be controlled by the same person – thus this type of boat requires at least two and sometimes three people in the middle to do the job of a single 'pitman'.

These differences make this section a little less structured than the comments relating to the bowman, but even so there are still definable jobs to be done and in most cases it is probably not too hard to decide the type of yacht that may apply to you and how the general roles will fit into your own sailing situation. I have therefore split the section, roughly at least, into the 'mastman' and the 'pit'.

The Mastman

The crew working at the mast will be in control of all the halyards at that point, ensuring that when they are used or stored they do not get twisted. During any sail change he will be sweating the new halyard up and will often assist the bowman with genoa take-downs. He will also be controlling the inboard end of the spinnaker pole. He may also be dealing with tripping the pole open during gybes.

On good sized yachts, some of these tasks require a fair amount of brute strength, especially sweating halyards to the top. This particular job can be critical for a good spinnaker set when the sail must get to the top without a pause. For this to work properly it is necessary to have the halyards exiting from the mast as high as reasonably possible – at least two metres above the deck – and to have the pitman tailing efficiently. One common mistake is to see the mastman pulling the halyard up a couple of feet at a time rather than using his full height, stretching up to grip the rope and then pulling smoothly down almost to the deck before stretching up once again. When the load becomes too great for straightforward pulling, the halyard should be sweated out from the mast, pulling out about halfway between the halyard exit and the deck and working in close liaison with the pitman who is tailing the rope. Sailing gloves are essential for this part of the job, especially if either wire/rope or Spectra with the sheath removed is being used for the halyards. Either of these can cut into your hands quite badly.

Apart from simple upper body strength, height can also be an advantage for this job. The taller you are, the more halyard you are able to pull up in one body movement. That is not to say that shorter people cannot make good mastmen, but simply that the job is simpler if you are tall. Tall crews have other advantages too, they can reach the spinnaker pole more easily (more important on larger yachts) and will also be able to reach further up the mainsail luff tape when reefing. If you are working in the position of mast and want to do any physical training then it is principally upper body strength which is required together with strong fingers, although as with all crewing positions a good general level of fitness is also a great advantage.

The inboard end of the spinnaker pole will need adjusting to keep it horizontal. Some yachts save weight by only having two or three rings on the front of the mast for pole attachment but most will have a sliding track of some kind. Whichever system is in use it is important to get to know the approximate heights for various wind angles and also the optimum height for gybing. When adjusting a pole with compression load on it, the easiest order is to be to adjust the inboard end first, taking the pole from level, and then to raise or lower the outboard end later. One problem often encountered with the set up at the mast is for the rope controlling the inboard end not to jam easily and for the pole to fall down (or be forced up) under load. If this is your area of work then it is up to you to make the system

Photo 2.4 The mastman using his full body weight to get the headsail aloft fast. In the final stages of the hoist he will be sweating the halyard, pulling it outward from the mast, and here the synchronisation between him and his pitman will be vital.

work. If, as with Sigma 38s, the problem is simply that the rope size is too large for the cleats, then this can be changed for rope of smaller diameter and the problem should be solved.

As well as having the mast marked for inboard end heights, the pole lift should also be marked if using dip pole gybes. This allows the pole to be dropped to the right height to swing over the guard-rail but inside the forestay. I like to have a cleat on the mast for this purpose, the uphaul can be jammed in this and the correct amount of slack put in the system from the cockpit before jamming there as well. As the pole is tripped off the guy, the uphaul is pulled from the cleat on the mast and it will automatically fall to the right level. Incidentally, beware of topping the pole too quickly after a gybe – it is important that the tip of the pole never goes above the foot of the spinnaker until the guy is right back, otherwise it is all too easy to poke the pole through the spinnaker!

When reefing it will be the mastman's job to pull down on the luff of the mainsail and hook on the tack fitting. Once again this will need to be done in conjunction with the pitman who will normally be letting the halyard down to a predetermined mark, re-tensioning it and then pulling in the reefing clew line.

The Pit and Halyards

This job calls for someone who is well organised and who is able to think ahead to at least the next manoeuvre – if not to the one after that. Gloves are again essential; if not used, there is a real danger of getting serious rope burns, especially as a spinnaker halyard is released.

Size is not too important for this position and in fact it is a positive disadvantage to be too heavy since there will be many times that the pitman is one of the first off the rail. Reasonable arm strength and good arm muscle stamina is called for and it is worth doing some work to achieve strength in these areas. Another attribute which is invaluable is a well developed sense of timing. Especially when dropping halyards, a split second too late and the sail might not come down, too early and the sail will still be full and impossible to pull inboard.

Before a halyard is released it must always be prepared, usually by flaking in a figure of eight shape to prevent kinks developing as it runs free. Most pitmen will let the tail of a halyard drop loosely down the hatch when hoisting and then flake it prior to a drop or alternatively they may flake it directly onto the top of the halyard winch if it is a boat with several individual winches rather than a bank of stoppers and multi-task winches. If a halyard is to run free when it is released, there must be no turns left on the winch as these would induce too much friction. With stoppers this is no problem because the stoppers can always be closed to halt the drop if required. With a rope coming straight off a winch it is rather more difficult and it is prudent to keep a single turn on the winch for windy spinnaker drops in case something goes wrong.

One method of preparing the yacht for quick and easy sail drops that is often seen on match racers and which is probably best used inshore, is to have some sail-ties or ropes tied across the yacht below deck and about one metre forward of the hatch. The halyards can be thrown over and forward of these ropes which then act as a sort of fairleads for the halyards on a drop. They also keep the cabin sole at the base of the companionway clear of ropes.

When dropping a spinnaker the most common mistake is for the halyard man to be over-cautious. If the halyard is lowered slowly, the spinnaker will almost inevitably stay full of wind and will be a real problem to recover. If, on the other hand, the halyard is allowed to run free, this will collapse the spinnaker which will make life much easier for the recovery crew. When dropping small spinnakers (say on yachts up to about ten metres long) it is perfectly safe to blow the whole halyard away, but on larger yachts it may be necessary to do the drop in two parts. First blow about two thirds of the halyard and then check it to prevent the head of the sail taking a swim. Once the crew have recovered the bulk of the sail, the final part of the halyard can then be

Photo 2.5 The pitman is carefully flaking down a halyard on the side-deck to make sure that it will run freely on the drop.

Photo 2.5A The pit demands a methodical and tidy mind if the mass of control lines are not to become hopelessly tangled.

lowered. Gloves and/or good stoppers are essential for this to work. The only time this method should not be used is after a peel when the spinnaker will have been tripped away at the bow and will be flying out aft. In this case the halyard needs to be lowered under control.

Really good technique is required to tail a halyard which is being sweated up by the mastman. It is vital that you keep up with him otherwise he could be left holding a sail under load without the assistance of winches or cleats – rarely a good idea. Also, if slack develops between the mastman and the pit it will often end with a snarl up at the turning block by the base of the mast. The most efficient technique seems to be to grasp the rope with one hand at a time and to swing that arm out sideways in a wide arc with your elbows high and wide, before taking hold with the other hand. This produces a movement

Photo 2.6 Rapid and long sweeps of the arms are required to keep up with the mastman as he pulls the halyard during a hoist. Here the pitman is in the best position for the job; he has plenty of elbow room and is unlikely to KO any cockpit crew.

three turns on the winch from the start.

It is most important to have all the halyards marked so that both the pitman and mastman can see when the sail is fully hoisted without having to look aloft. A mark on the halyard corresponding to another on the mast is often the simplest solution although another option for genoa halyards is to have both the luff of the sail and the luff groove marked about two metres above the deck – when they line up the sail is fully hoisted.

The tensioning of a genoa halyard should not be attempted unless some load comes off the head of the sail. This is achieved by either the trimmer easing the sheet or by the helmsman luffing – or both. If you wind the sail up when it is fully loaded, then delamination at the head will eventually be the result.

To conclude this section, both mastman and pitman need to work closely with each other and especially with the bowman. Good organisation is called for as is a keen sense of timing. Although often thought of as 'just middle of the boat crew', both these positions are vital for the successful completion of most manoeuvres.

which is potentially lethal for any other crew member who happens to be too close but does get the rope in quickly. Normally, tailing of spinnaker halyards will be done with the stopper closed and just one turn around the winch but for a genoa halyard where it is almost certain that you will need to wind it up to the correct height after the initial hoist, some time can be saved by having two or even

Fig 2.6
Luff Groove/
Sail — Hoist
Position

The Headsail Trimmer

So far in this chapter, the crew positions which we have looked at have been fairly physical with a set series of parameters to learn. Now we will look at the task of a genoa trimmer. This position involves a certain amount of relatively basic skill that is not difficult to learn but to excel at this task will take a great deal of experience if optimum performance is to be obtained from a particular sail in a variety of conditions. The headsail trimmer will be working in conjunction with the mainsail trimmer and the helmsman to transfer the available power in the most effective possible manner. It is also very important to be able to look at a sail and decide how it could be improved and then convey that in a language that the sailmaker will understand.

Before getting into the detail of trimming let us consider for a moment the required general attributes necessary for the job. He must be a good team player – his job is part of the overall power package of the sails and he must work closely in conjunction with the mainsail trimmer and the helmsman if the boat is to achieve its optimum speed. He must understand the theory of sails and how they create the driving force that powers the boat and he must also be prepared to concentrate hard for long periods. Strength is not particularly important and this makes trimming a good job for female crew – especially as they often have better concentration than their male counterparts.

Headsail Trimming Upwind

Here the trimmer will be looking at the overall sail shape, both in isolation and also in conjunction with the mainsail and will be adjusting its shape as appropriate for the conditions. The basic principles are quite simple and start with the choice of headsail to suit the prevailing wind and sea conditions. In general terms it is usual nowadays to change

at least to the No3 before putting anything more than a flattening reef in the mainsail and the actual size of genoa to be used will be determined mainly by the angle of heel when properly trimmed – you will need to know the boat's characteristics before this decision can be made.

The controls that you will be using as a headsail trimmer will be dealt with in detail in the sail trimming chapter, but a little repetition here will do no harm:-

The halyard

This controls the luff tension and therefore the position of maximum draft in the sail. As the wind increases, so the sail is stretched back and thus halyard tension must be increased to maintain draft at about an average of 40-45% of the distance between the luff and the leech.

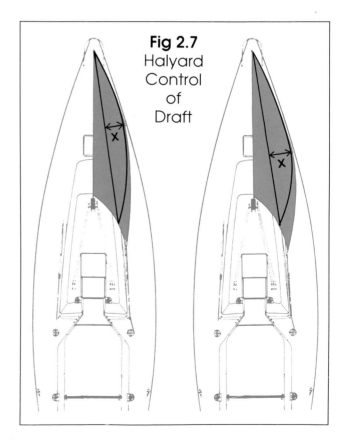

Fig 2.7
Halyard
Control
of
Draft

When calling for the halyard to be tightened remember that the load must be taken off the sail if damage is to be avoided. This can either be achieved by easing the sheet, luffing or a combination of both.

In flat water the helmsman will be able to sail in a narrower groove than is possible in waves In these smooth conditions it is feasible to use slightly less halyard tension, making the entry flatter and allowing a higher pointing angle but this also makes it harder to steer to the sail. As wave size increases for a particular wind strength, so the sail will require more halyard tension, making the entry rounder and easier to steer by. It will also make the helmsman sail a little freer in order to keep the tell-tales flying.

As a general rule, Kevlar sails need less adjustment to the halyard than Mylar/Dacron sails and these in turn need less adjustment than plain Dacron ones. This is because the high technology cloths stretch less and are therefore not affected to any great degree by changes in wind strength.

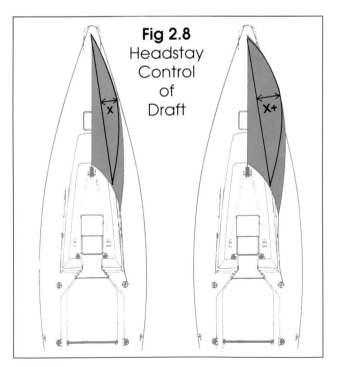

Fig 2.8
Headstay
Control
of
Draft

Headstay Tension

The next control that the trimmer must consider is the amount of headstay sag. Whereas the halyard controls the position of maximum draft in the sail, the headstay sag controls the actual amount of draft. As the headstay sags more, the distance from the luff to leech decreases and so the sail becomes fuller. Conversely, when the headstay is tightened, the distance from luff to leech increases and there is less draft in the sail. Because the headstay sags backwards in the middle, this works in exactly the opposite way to mast bend with the mainsail.

With a masthead rig, headstay sag will be controlled with the fixed backstay. Tightening the backstay will move the top of the mast back and will therefore also tighten the headstay – so long as the mast is not allowed to go too far out of column. On fractionally rigged boats, the headstay is normally controlled by the runners, although on some simple rigs with untapered topmast sections the backstay will have an effect as well.

If sailing with a really simple fractional rig with swept back spreaders but without runners, it is mainly cap shroud tension that determines headstay sag. This means that it becomes very important to adjust the cap shroud tension for differing wind strengths. Many of these boats sail with their rigs too loose and thus with too much sag in their forestays. As an example it was very noticeable at one recent regatta that one boat was dramatically faster than her sister-ships upwind and it was just as obvious that her rig tension was much greater, allowing her to point higher with less headstay sag.

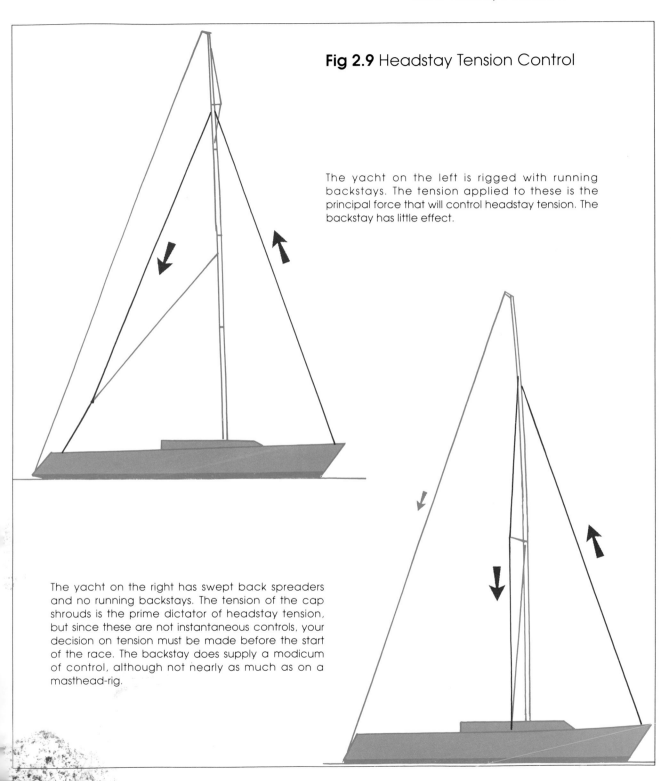

Fig 2.9 Headstay Tension Control

The yacht on the left is rigged with running backstays. The tension applied to these is the principal force that will control headstay tension. The backstay has little effect.

The yacht on the right has swept back spreaders and no running backstays. The tension of the cap shrouds is the prime dictator of headstay tension, but since these are not instantaneous controls, your decision on tension must be made before the start of the race. The backstay does supply a modicum of control, although not nearly as much as on a masthead-rig.

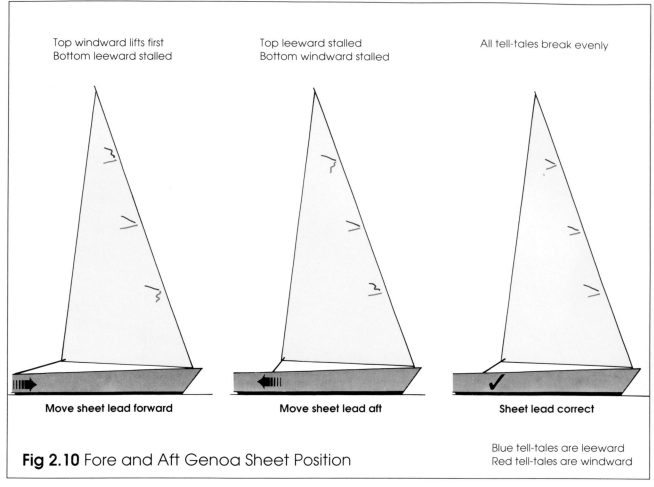

Top windward lifts first
Bottom leeward stalled

Top leeward stalled
Bottom windward stalled

All tell-tales break evenly

Move sheet lead forward

Move sheet lead aft

Sheet lead correct

Fig 2.10 Fore and Aft Genoa Sheet Position

Blue tell-tales are leeward
Red tell-tales are windward

Fore and Aft Sheet Position

The fore and aft sheet position of the genoa sheet controls the relative loads on the foot and leech of the headsail. Too far forward and the leech will be tight, the foot very loose and rounded and the top of the sail stalled. Too far aft and the reverse will happen, the foot will be stretched flat against the shroud base, the sail will have too much twist and the top will have fallen away to leeward and be flapping.

The way to position the sheet lead to approximately the correct location is simple enough – get the helmsman to sail on (say) the middle tell-tales and while these are set perfectly, look at the top and bottom tell-tales. If the top needs to be sheeted in harder then consider moving the lead forward a notch or two while if the leech looks very hard and the top tell-tales are stalled, the lead needs to moved aft.

It is important that the trimmer has an easy way of moving the sheet lead fore and aft. In an ideal world it should be possible to do this with a tackle system to allow adjustment while the sail is under full load, but failing that, a change-sheet led to a second fairlead car will allow quite simple changes in position. First take up the load on the change-sheet, then free off the genoa sheet itself and move the car, then take up the load on the proper sheet again – recheck the lead position and finally remove the change-sheet.

Photo 2.7 A straightforward system of moving the fairlead car fore and aft along its track. In practice the car only needs to be pulled forwards and the line running inside the sheet and to the front of the track turns round a block and then back to the car, thus providing a facility of pulling the car forward. The natural desire of the sheet to rise will pull the car aft when the line is released.

Sheet Tension

This is the most basic but also the hardest of the headsail controls for the trimmer to get right. The correct setting is the one which allows the helmsman to achieve the maximum Vmg for a given wind speed. In general terms the tighter the sheet, the higher will be the pointing angle – but at the expense of boat speed.

The trimmer needs a system for reproducing a particular sheet tension and this is normally done by marking the spreaders with tape at about 25mm intervals and then using these marks as a guide to the distance between the leech of the sail and the spreader tip. A good trimmer will be liaising carefully with the helmsman to ensure that he has not oversheeted the sail but at the same time has got it in as far as is possible without killing boat speed.

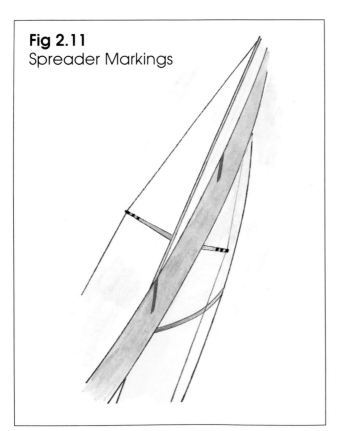

Fig 2.11
Spreader Markings

In waves it will not be possible to sail so high as when the water is flat and this means that the trim will need to be a little softer in waves. If the yacht goes through a particularly rough patch (or a speed-boat wake or similar) then the sheet will should be eased slightly, but if very high pointing is desired it must be trimmed in hard.

After a tack, the apparent wind speed and the boat speed will both be down, making it important to trim the sail a little eased until speed has built up to normal figures. Ideally, the sail should also be powered up coming out of the tack with less headstay tension and the sheet lead further forward than normal. Once the yacht has accelerated to something near its normal speed the headstay can be tightened and the lead moved back to its usual position.

Inboard or Outboard Sheeting

The final headsail control is the athwartship position of the sheet lead. The further inboard the lead is placed, the narrower the sheeting angle and thus the higher it is possible to point. But the other effect of this is that as the sheet lead comes inboard, so the genoa backwinds the mainsail more and more as the slot is closed. On most cruiser racers the other problem with very narrow sheeting bases is that their relatively long spreaders do not allow the sail to be sheeted in too close at the bottom because the sail will hit the spreaders or shrouds higher up.

In general terms the genoa should be sheeted inboard until either the wind fairs to a reach or until the yacht is becoming overpowered with the sail combination in use. Especially with large overlapping headsails, the mainsail trimmer will find it impossible to lose power by dropping the traveller down the track if the slot is narrow. Once the boat is becoming overpowered, it is worth considering moving the lead aft (to twist the top of the sail more) and outboard to open the slot and allow the main to be freed in the gusts.

Photo 2.8 When the boat has cracked-off onto a reach and the helmsman is sailing a course rather than sailing by the wind, the headsail trimmer must concentrate totally on the tell-tales, sheeting in and out constantly to match the wind and the boats movements through the water. It is most efficient to use your hand clamped round the winch to lock the sheet (as shown) and forget about the cleat – it's faster. Also watch the athwartship sheeting angle if the wind comes aft or the driver bears away more. If there is a sudden change, check the compass or confirm that the course is still correct – some helmsmen like to look around!

Headsail Trimming on a Reach

Once the wind has freed and the boat is reaching with the headsail, the sheet must be eased. Now the helmsman will probably be sailing a compass course and the trimmer should keep the sail set to perfection – although there has to be a bit of latitude here with large boats since the wind can change faster than it is possible to alter the trim and the helmsman must therefore adjust the steering to help.

Another effect is that when the sheet is eased a little, the initial effect is to free the leech far more than the foot of the sail, causing the sail to twist off in an unacceptable way. This means that as the sheet is eased, it must also

Photo 2.9 As the wind frees on a reach the sheet lead should be moved outboard. Here a snatch-block has been clipped to a slide on the toe-rail and a reaching sheet is ready to clip on to the sail.

be moved forward to maintain the leech tension and prevent excessive twist. It is likely that the lead will also need to be moved outboard as the wind frees more.

By the time the lead has been moved out to the side of the yacht, it is probable that you will have transferred onto a reaching sheet, perhaps through a snatch-block on the toe-rail. It is usually best if this can be trimmed on a windward winch because by now the mainsail will also have been eased and will make the tell-tales on the genoa very hard to see from leeward. Apart from this, trimming from windward puts weight in the right place.

As the wind frees, the stretch back on the sail cloth decreases and so the draft will move forward unless the halyard is eased a little to compensate. As a guide, try to keep the point of maximum draft about forty-five per cent of the way back from the luff. If the boat is under-powered now that she is reaching, ease the runner or backstay as appropriate to allow the headstay to sag more and thus power up the genoa.

Headsail Trimmer – Tacking

During a tack, one trimmer will be letting off the old sheet while the new trimmer will be sheeting in the new one. If you are letting off it is vital to avoid kinks forming in the loose sheet and becoming caught in turning blocks. To avoid this, first prepare the sheet for tacking by flaking it roughly (not coiling). Then as the boat is turned, take one or two turns off the winch before throwing off the remainder and always leave half a turn on the winch so that the winch itself acts to remove kinks as the rope feeds out.

If doing the pulling in of the new sheet, remember not to sheet it too hard until the speed builds after the tack, then finally wind it in the last few inches once up to speed. I find the most efficient way to tail a sheet on most boats is for the tailer to take his rope right across the cockpit and up to the new windward side-deck, allowing plenty of room for the trimmer/grinder to get at the winch and also keeping his weight as high as possible.

Photo 2.10 The boat and crew are set up for optimum two-sail reaching in breezy conditions. All the crew weight is to weather including the headsail trimmer. He is trimming with a reaching sheet that has been led outboard and replaced the usual sheet which remains loaded on the leeward winch, although redundant. The sheet in use has been taken via a turning block, across the cockpit and to the windward winch. The trimmer should be able to see all the tell-tales from top to bottom of the luff so that he can evaluate both sheet tension and sheet lead position.

Photo 2.11 All is not as it appears! This boat has suddenly decided to luff away from the shore to protect its wind from following boats or for some other tactical reason. The spinnaker trimmer braces himself on the side-deck by the shrouds to keep the kite pulling. The guy needs tension to bring the tack of the spinnaker to windward of the headstay. A trimmer may find himself braced at this awkward angle for hours on end during an offshore race – both playing the sheet and keeping his balance.

The Spinnaker Trimmer

To trim a spinnaker efficiently requires a mind that can obliterate every thought other than keeping 'the bag on edge'. The fundamentals of trimming the sail are not too difficult to learn, but the ability to concentrate and keep the sail flying to its optimum for hour after hour calls for real dedication. There will be no chance for sight-seeing or looking at the competition. (It is perhaps for this reason, that I have found girls well suited to the task.) If the boat is large enough to warrant a winch and a person to grind it, then the spinnaker trimmer does not need to be overly strong but stamina is a vital prerequisite. On smaller boats it is unlikely that the services of a winch grinder will be available in all but the strongest of winds and the more violent movement of a smaller boat will demand strength and balance in addition to stamina.

The trimmer should call the whole sail in addition to trimming the sheet. This means talking to the person on the guy to maintain the correct pole to wind angle, to the mastman to keep pole height adjusted and to the helmsman about the current requirements of boat speed versus angle. It also means that the trimmer must stand in a position to be able to see the whole sail and not the luff alone. If running downwind in light or moderate breezes it is vital that the trimmer understands target angles and target speeds and is a good communicator in order to get the helmsman to sail the right angles. When sailing on a reach on a gusty day, the trimmer must understand the control problems which the helmsman will be experiencing and be ready to dump the sheet if all else fails and the boat shows signs of a broach.

Spinnaker Trimmer's Equipment

When reaching, the trimmer will often find himself wedged against the shrouds so that the all important luff is visible. On this point of sailing the loads on the sheet are cruellest and the luff is at such an acute angle that the neck is almost permanently bent backwards and during the daytime Sod's Law often dictates that the spinnaker luff is in line with the sun. Even if this is not the case, gazing upwards is always a strain on the eyes and dark sunglasses and a wind proof sun hat can alleviate the worst elements of maintaining this position.

Good sailing gloves are an absolute necessity and at night a good torch will be invaluable, even though you may need a third hand to aim it when on a reach!

Spinnaker Trim

The fundamentals of spinnaker trim are the control of pole height, guy trim (to square the pole), sheet angle and sheet tension.

Pole Height

Adjustment of pole height achieves two things. When the pole is lowered it tightens the luff of the sail and moves the draft further forward. (In exactly the same way as tightening the halyard does with a genoa.) This is why the pole needs to be much lower on a reach (when the wind is blowing the draft aft in the sail) than on a run. Lowering the pole also tightens the luff itself and will tend to stabilise the sail and this can be an advantage in very windy conditions. However, it must be appreciated that in general terms, if the pole is too low on a run, the sail will be less powerful and will be theoretically slower. Therefore, on a run it is normal to let the pole rise until the two clews are virtually level.

A good guide for correct pole height is to look at the point of the sail where the luff curls first when the sheet is eased. Ideally it should break first at the join between the vertical panels and the rounded shoulders (at the bottom of the radial panels on a radial headed sail). If the point of initial curl is higher than this, the pole is probably too high and vice versa if the spinnaker curls lower down. (See Fig 2.12)

In most situations the pole should be as near horizontal as possible. This gives it the maximum effective length and will keep the spinnaker as far away from the mainsail as possible, which is always good. (A tip when calling for the pole to be raised or lowered is to ensure that the inboard end is always adjusted first, since this avoids the mastman having a bow and arrow situation to deal with.)

Another tip which is worth noting, is to mark the mast for average pole heights for close a reach, a broad reach and Vmg running. These marks will not necessarily be the optimum heights but should give both the trimmer and other crew a starting point when the spinnaker is first hoisted.

(See Photos 2.12 & 2.13)

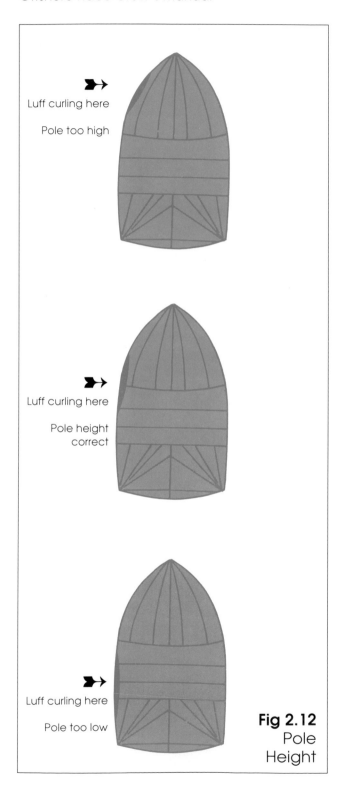

Luff curling here

Pole too high

Luff curling here

Pole height
correct

Luff curling here

Pole too low

Fig 2.12
Pole
Height

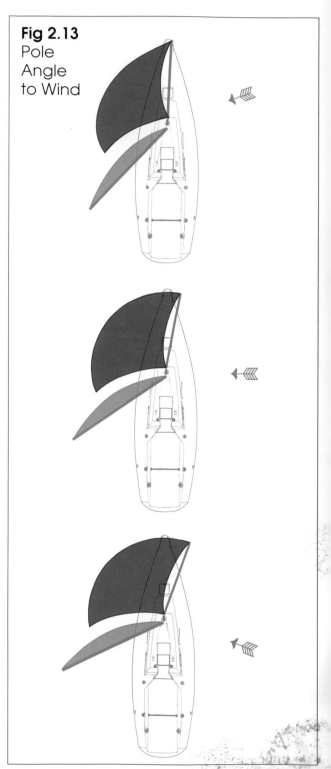

Fig 2.13
Pole
Angle
to Wind

Photo 2.12 Here the pole height looks OK. The centre seam of the spinnaker is vertical.

Photo 2.13 The tack and clew of the spinnaker are level – pole height right.

Squaring the Pole

A common error often seen is when the pole is set too far forward, especially on shy reaches in gusty conditions. When on a broad reach, perhaps with the wind aft of 130°, the pole should be roughly square to the apparent wind. If then you consider the other extreme, when sailing as close to the wind as possible and with an apparent wind angle of about 75° and the pole on the headstay, it is obvious that it is impossible to maintain this 90° pole angle

and that in fact the pole must be over squared by about 15°. As the wind frees from 75° this over squaring of the pole should only be gradually reduced, so that by the time the apparent wind is on the beam the pole might still be 10° over square, reducing down to nothing by the time the apparent wind has freed to about 110°.

A good guide to determine whether the pole is squared sufficiently is to look at the luff of the sail. If it is vertical from the pole up to the

Photo 2.14 On a spinnaker hoist, the trimmer should initially pull on a little sheet to pull the clew clear and aft of the bag. He will then wait until the sail is hoisted before sheeting-on to get it pulling.

shoulders the guy is about right, if the luff leans to leeward from the end of the pole then the guy is probably squared too far aft. The reverse is true if the luff appears to be going to windward from the pole end.

Sheet Lead

The sheet lead for the spinnaker normally turns near the back of the boat. This will need tweaking down in two circumstances – firstly when running quite square in ordinary conditions to stop the leech opening too much (analogous to reducing twist in a genoa) and secondly when running in heavy airs to choke

the spinnaker down and keep it under control. In heavy airs it also prevents excessive twist in the gusts which could otherwise induce heel to windward and start a rhythmic death roll.

Sheet Tension

Finally we come to sheet tension. This is the line that is being controlled directly by the trimmer and should always (nearly) be eased until the luff of the sail is just starting to curl. Any harder in than this and the sail is stalled – any further out and the whole sail will collapse. Constant trimming will be needed in order to keep the sail at this optimum point.

Photo 2.15 As the spinnaker reaches full hoist, the trimmer sheets-on to fill the sail. He will then play the sheet to keep the luff on-edge.

Spinnaker Trimmer – Hoisting

When hoisting the spinnaker, the trimmer must be careful not to sheet on until the sail is at full hoist; a prematurely filled spinnaker can take layers of skin from the hands pulling up the halyard and result in both spinnaker and trimmer receiving a ducking! However, if the sail is allowed to flog as it is being hoisted, there is a good chance of it going up with a twist. The ideal middle course, especially if the sail is not in stops, is for the sheet to be trimmed on briefly as the sail comes out of the bag – this opens the foot out and prevents twisting – then before the spinnaker has set the sheet is eased again so that it flaps until completely hoisted. This technique calls for good timing and close co-ordination between the trimmer and his grinder. The guy should always be squared very quickly, at least until the tack is at the headstay. Once the sail is up the guy must be squared back to its proper place – but it is all too easy to square back too far unless the course and angle have been discussed before the hoist.

Spinnaker Trimmer – Gybing

During a spinnaker gybe, the helmsman should be steering the boat under the kite while the trimmer keeps it full at all times. In most situations (until you get onto boats larger than about twelve metres) it is best for one trimmer to take both sheets during the gybe itself. In this way, one person can control both clews and there is never one clew fighting against the other. If gybing from a run to a run, the pole will only need to be squared back slightly but in any case the new sheet must be good and tight before the pole is tripped or taken off the mast. Once the pole has been gybed, the old sheet must be eased as the guy is wound in. A potentially disastrous fault is to let the old sheet go completely which allows the spinnaker to fly forward and collapse.

Spinnaker Trimmer – Float Drop

In a float drop, the pole is tripped away from the guy when the yacht is still about two lengths from the leeward mark. This is only done in light to moderate conditions when it is necessary to gybe around the leeward mark and yet keep the spinnaker set for as long as possible. When the pole is tripped away the spinnaker must be kept flying or there is no point to the pole drop and so the trimmer once again will be trimming the sail using both sheets in the same way as is done during a gybe.(Practise two sheet control of the spinnaker away from a racing situation – it is actually very easy.) Ensure that you have taken up tension on the lazy sheet before the pole is tripped away or once again the spinnaker will lurch forward and collapse.

Spinnaker Trimming in Waves

The level of concentration required to keep the boat at maximum speed rises dramatically when sailing downwind in sizeable waves. Every time the yacht accelerates down the front of a wave the apparent wind will move forward and the pole must therefore be eased and the sheet trimmed in. Conversely, when the boat slows at the bottom of a wave or starts climbing up the back of the wave ahead, the apparent wind will increase and move aft, making it important to square the pole and ease the sheet. In marginal handling conditions great care needs to be taken to stay in time with the boat and to work closely with the helmsman in order to avoid broaching, either to windward or even worse to leeward.

Spinnaker Trimming in Light Airs

Sailing downwind in light airs calls for an excellent rapport between the helmsman and the spinnaker trimmer. There is a constant compromise between angle and boat speed and even with the best polar table and target speed to work from, the best result is always hard to achieve.

In these circumstances, the trimmer is the person who can best feel what is happening, through the sensitive pressures on the sheet. I like to sail in these very light airs with the trimmer calling 'up' or 'down' to the helm, as the pressure builds and fades. With practice, it is not hard to sense what amounts to good pressure (and therefore reasonable speed), once there is pressure in the sail, the helm can sail a little lower, once pressure starts to drop, say in a lull, he must sail higher at least for a time. If the boat boasts sophisticated instrumentation with performance functions the trimmer can gauge feel to figures to choose the right calls.

The Grinder

The winch grinder's task is very different to that of the trimmer. He needs to be fit and strong, especially in his upper body and his muscles need to be able to deliver huge amounts of power in relatively short bursts, often with little break between effort.

The skills needed to be an efficient grinder are fairly simple to learn, although most of the best grinders are good crewmen in other positions as well. He must know how to put a rope onto a winch so that riding turns do not occur, how to put in a handle, both efficiently and quickly and how to exert just enough force to do the job without exhausting himself.

Putting turns on the winch correctly usually means not putting too many on the winch until the load starts to build up – three turns are normally sufficient initially. Inserting the handle sounds too easy to be worth mentioning but in fact I have watched all sorts of people waste time by not being organised in their approach. The most important thing is to be holding the handle by the shank and not by the handle itself. If it is a locking handle it is often easier to get into the winch if the lock is pressed across with your thumb at the same time.

Use of body weight to augment upper body strength is important. To exert maximum power the grinder should be positioned right over the winch in an attitude that feels comfortable and where he is braced against the movements of the boat. When tacking, he should remember that the main winching will be done after the yacht is on the new tack and ensure that he is balanced appropriately. Obviously an understanding of the winches themselves is also important. If using multi-geared winches the gear changes must be smooth and fast.

Grinding with pedestal winches sometimes found on larger yachts demands its own technique. The greatest problem for crew not used to grinding in unison with a partner on crank handles is to forget to hold on tight in order to avoid being thrown off. If you ever do lose your grip with one or both hands, the only way to get back on the handles without either stopping or risking a broken wrist, is to place your hand(s) on your partners shoulder(s) and work your own hand down his arm until you reach the winch. In this way you will be able to keep in time with him.

Letting the sheet fly is another skill which is often not applied correctly. If there are more than three turns on the winch before the tack is called, the additional turns should carefully be unwound as the load starts to come off the winch. When the sheet is let fly, the last three turns should be spun quickly from the top of the winch. A frequent problem when letting fly is that of getting kinks running down the rope and becoming caught in the turning block. There are two things that should be done to prevent this. Firstly, the sheet needs to be flaked from the standing end every so often to remove any semi permanent kinks from the rope. Secondly, half a turn should be left around the winch when the sheet has been cast off, since this allows the winch to 'clean' the rope of kinks as it flies out. Do not try this last technique if using self tailing winches as it is highly probable that the sheet will get caught in the jammer at the top of the winch.

Working in unison with the trimmers is what winch grinding is all about. A good grinder can make a trimmer's job look easy, a bad or inattentive grinder can make even the best trimmer look pretty average. There should be good communication between the person tailing/trimming the rope and the grinder. Good partnerships use eye contact so that when the trimmer wants the sheet wound in, the grinder does not wait for a verbal request to grind, but will be doing it already. It is often possible for the grinder to watch the trimmer's arm muscles and grind as soon as they start to tension. In a tack, the trimmer should be able to tail in most of the slack sheet but it will help considerably if the winch is already turning before load comes on to the sheet. Slow

Photo 2.16 The grinder backs-up the spinnaker trimmer on the port cabin-top winch. Notice how he positions himself over the winch to generate power from his shoulders and brings his entire body weight to bear.

winding until the sail is through the fore triangle, followed by a sharp burst until it is in enough for initial post-tack acceleration is most efficient. The trimmer should call when to stop as it is not part of the grinder's job to be watching the leech of the sail – he should just be grinding.

The Mainsheet Trimmer

In my view, the job of the mainsheet trimmer is the most physically demanding on the yacht. Unlike most other tasks it is continuous and except on really small or very large yachts, strength and stamina are required to operate the sheet and traveller systems.

The ideal mainsheet man should be generally fit, fairly heavy and very strong, especially in the upper body and back areas. If you want to become a good mainsail trimmer, then in addition to learning the technical skills required, you should also to do some serious work in the gymnasium to build up stamina, weight and strength. Because the mainsail is such an important part of the driving force of the yacht, it must be trimmed properly at all times, not just for the first half hour of a race.

However it is important not to get the idea that a mainsheet trimmer only needs strength; he must also understand how the boat, sails and rig all work together and he should have excellent powers of concentration. Another important criterion for a good trimmer is the ability to work with others as part of the team. As we shall see later, the mainsheet trimmer must liaise closely with both the helmsman and the genoa trimmers in order to maximise performance.

So to sum up, the ideal mainsheet man will be strong with good stamina, have good concentration and will be prepared to be one of the team.

Mast Tune – Prebend

As with the spinnaker trimmer, the mainsheet man must be calling all aspects of mainsail trim, not just the sheet. This involves adjusting the depth of the sail, the point of maximum draft, the amount of twist and the angle to the wind of the whole sail.

The amount of depth or draft in the sail is controlled in two ways. Mast bend is the chief control plus the use of the clew outhaul for the bottom part of the sail. When setting a

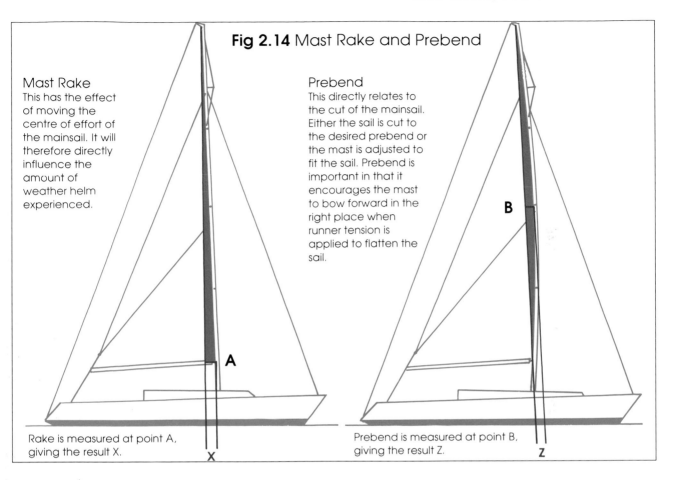

Fig 2.14 Mast Rake and Prebend

Mast Rake
This has the effect of moving the centre of effort of the mainsail. It will therefore directly influence the amount of weather helm experienced.

Prebend
This directly relates to the cut of the mainsail. Either the sail is cut to the desired prebend or the mast is adjusted to fit the sail. Prebend is important in that it encourages the mast to bow forward in the right place when runner tension is applied to flatten the sail.

Rake is measured at point A, giving the result X.

Prebend is measured at point B, giving the result Z.

mainsail up, the first task is to get the mast tune correct for the sail. This is mainly about prebend which is controlled by a combination of mast heel position, deck chocking and forestay length. Ideally, the sailmaker will ask how much prebend you want to sail with before designing the sail, but in most cases we need to set the mast to suit the sail which we have.

Prebend increases the distance from luff to leech and therefore more bend creates less shape in the sail. With fractional rigged yachts, prebend will only affect the bottom two thirds of the sail because anything above the hounds will not be altered by runner tension. With a masthead yacht, prebend is effective all the way to the top of the sail. In either case, too much bend and the sail will be too flat, too

little and it will always be baggy whatever else you try. In an extreme case of too much prebend, the sail will exhibit characteristic creases from the clew to the area of the lower spreader. This is simply because there is insufficient cloth in the sail to accommodate the bend in the mast.

Given one mainsail and the option to change rig tuning from day to day, you would sail with more prebend as the wind increases. In most cases however, boats set the rig as a compromise for any weather conditions. If you should wish to alter the amount of prebend, the two easy ways to increase it are either to lengthen the forestay (often not allowed without re-rating) or re-chock at deck level with less chocks in front and more behind the mast.

Mainsail Trimming Upwind

Upwind the task is truly continuous. The mainsheet normally controls the leech tension and the traveller alters the angle of the sail relative to the fore and aft line of the yacht. As a preliminary rough guide, the sheet should be pulled in until the top batten is more or less in line with the boom when sighted from below. A more accurate method is to have a tell-tale at the leech end of the top batten pocket and to sheet in until it is almost, but not quite stalled. When oversheeted, the air flow will run along the windward side of the sail but there will be turbulence to leeward, particularly towards the leech and so the top tell-tale will disappear around the back of the sail into the stalled air. If under-sheeted, the top tell-tale will stream back from the sail continuously. The correct amount of sheet tension in most cases, is achieved when this top tell-tale is streaming some of the time but occasionally disappears. If the need is for the boat to foot fast then the tell-tale should stream almost continuously while if high pointing is required it should be stalled for most of the time.

Once the mainsheet has been initially adjusted, the sail is then trimmed up or down on the traveller to give the desired amount of weather helm – about 4° – 6° angle on a tiller or about an eighth turn on a wheel is usually right – setting the traveller higher up the track causes increased weather helm and vice versa. In light winds it will not be possible to induce any real weather helm and in this situation the traveller should be positioned to put the boom itself on the centreline of the yacht.

When the wind increases in a gust, the sail will stretch more and thus the sheet should be tightened to maintain the correct leech tension, and at the same time it will make it necessary to drop the traveller down the track a little.

The overall shape of the sail also needs to be altered as the wind increases or drops, but how you achieve this will depend upon the controls that are available. As the wind picks up, it will be necessary to flatten the sail progressively by tightening on the clew outhaul, until the clew is at the black band. Thereafter, if a flatter shape is required in the lower third of the sail, the flattening reef should be used. The middle of the sail can be flattened by inducing more mast bend in the centre. On a fractional rig this is done by easing the checkstays and tightening the runners. Easing the checkstays allows the middle of the mast to move further forward and tightening the runners pulls the mast back more at the hounds, thus inducing more prebend. The runners also compress the spar and make it easier to bend. With a masthead rig the same result can be achieved by tightening the fixed backstay to compress the mast and increase prebend, while easing the runner and checkstay allows the middle of the mast to move forward.

On a fractional rig, the fixed backstay controls mast bend in the upper part of the spar, so tightening this will bend the top of the mast and flatten the top third of the sail. The fixed backstay and runners on a fractionally rigged boat and the fixed backstay on a masthead boat will also tighten the forestay, which in turn flattens the genoa – one of the reasons why both headsail and mainsail trimmers need to work together as part of the overall team.

Luff tension is the final part of the equation. The position of maximum draft (sail curvature) in a mainsail needs to be about half way between luff and leech; this is controlled by halyard and/or Cunningham tension. As with the genoa, when the wind increases, it will physically stretch the sail backwards away from the mast and must therefore be dragged back to the middle of the sail with more luff tension. When the wind dies or the apparent wind moves further aft, there will be less tendency for the sail to stretch backwards and therefore less luff tension will be required.

Fig 2.15 Mainsail Leech Tension

By sighting up from under the boom it is possible to obtain the correct leech tension.

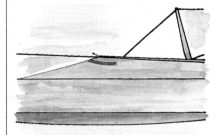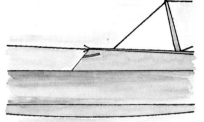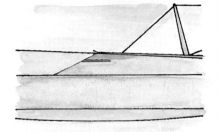

Too much leech tension — the top batten is hooking up to windward.

Ease the sheet a little.

Too little leech tension — the top batten is falling off to leeward

Pull in a little more sheet.

Correct — the top batten is in line with the boom.

So, the mainsheet trimmer has many controls to utilize, or at least call for their adjustment. Clew outhaul and mast bend to control the depth of the sail, luff tension to control the position of that depth, sheet tension to alter the leech tension and the traveller to give increase or decrease of weather helm as required by the helmsman. Obviously not all boats will have immediate response controls for every aspect of mainsail trim, but the racier and more tweaky the boat, then the more important it will be to get it all right.

On some simply rigged yachts where the traveller is not really long enough or where it locks up in windy weather when there is a lot of sheet tension, it is possible to make use of a powerful kicking strap (boom vang) to help control leech tension. This can be tightened to hold the boom down and this then releases some load from the traveller which may allow it to be played more effectively. In extreme cases, perhaps with no traveller at all, it can be worth using the kicking strap as the only leech tension control and then use the mainsheet itself to move the sail up and down for weather helm control. I have found that Sigma 33s respond well to this form of 'vang-sheeting' since their travellers are notoriously inefficient in gusty weather. There are dangers however. The first of these is that a considerable load is placed on the goose-neck fitting and on the boom itself and secondly, it is vital when vang-sheeting to release some of the vang tension *before* bearing away. If this is not done the boom will be forcing the middle of the mast sideways as the sheet is eased and it can cause mast failure.

Photo 2.17 The mainsheet trimmer often needs another pair of hands – here he is adjusting the backstay tension which controls the sail's shape at the head. The primary mainsail control lines, traveller and fine-tune sheet rest on his knee ready for immediate action.

Fig 2.16 Mainsail Control Systems

1 Mainsheet
Controls leech tension on the wind and sail angle off the wind.

2 Traveller
This dictates the angle of the sail to the wind within the scope of its length.

3 Kicking Strap
Controls leech tension when off the wind and in cases where the mainsheet is not effective.

4 Cunningham
This will bring the draft forward in the sail as the wind increases.
(Likewise the halyard until the black band at the masthead is reached.)

5 Clew Outhaul
Controls the depth of the lower third of the sail.

6 Flattener
This will flatten the lower part of the sail.

7 Running Backstay
Principally controls headstay sag —
also increases mast compression thus increasing mast bend.

8 Checkstay
Another mast bend control that prevents the mast bowing forward to excess, but which must be eased to create a flatter sail when the runner is applied.

9 Backstay
On this fractionally rigged boat this controls mast bend in the top part of the sail. On a masthead boat it would have a more significant effect on total sail shape.

10 Babystay
Really only used on fractional boats in rough weather to steady the mast. On some masthead boats it may be used to help pull the centre of the mast forward to create mast bend and therefore flatten the sail.

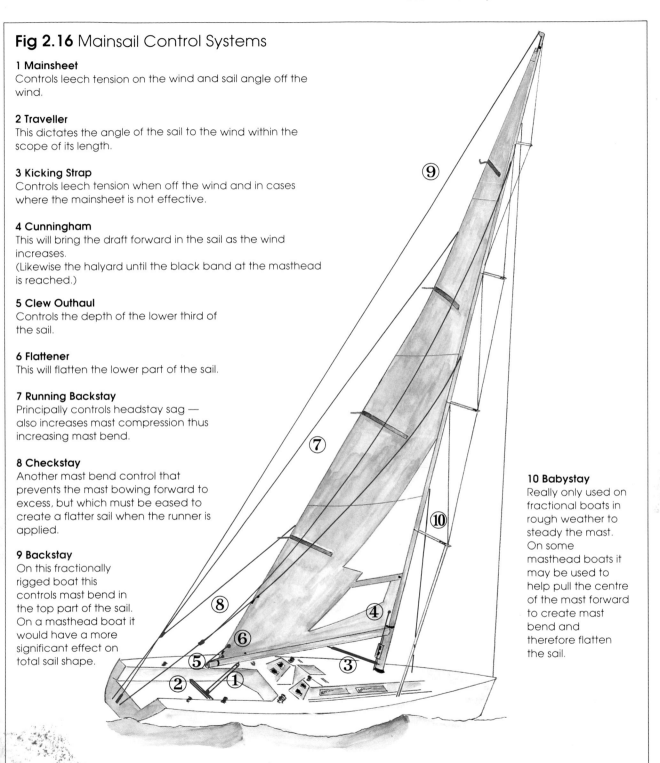

Mainsheet – Tacking

During a tack the apparent wind changes considerably and so the mainsail trim should be altered to suit. As the yacht turns towards the wind, the traveller is brought up to windward to keep the sail drawing for as long as possible and then as she bears away onto the new tack two things should happen at once. To start with, the traveller will need to be brought up sharply to the new high side as the wind changes sides in the sail and also the sheet will need to be eased slightly to take account of the reduction in apparent wind strength and a somewhat broader angle to the wind immediately after the tack. The sheet should then be gradually trimmed in to its 'normal' position as the yacht accelerates up to target speed. On windy days do not bother too much about the traveller but still try to ease the sheet a little – if you have a coarse/fine tune system then just dumping the fine tune is usually sufficient.

Mainsail Trim on a Reach

On a close to beam reach, the mainsail must still be trimmed constantly as it is still acting as a powerful aerofoil and most of the same trimming criteria still apply. Here, the traveller will be well eased and most leech tension will be controlled by the kicking strap. It is important not to over-vang the sail because it is quite easy to stall the sail completely and once again the top tell-tale provides the chief guide to leech tension. In this instance, the boat will by definition be footing fast and therefore the top tell-tale should be streaming aft virtually all the time. If it is stalled it will induce too much weather helm and the yacht will be slowed.

The sheet is then trimmed to reduce any flapping in the luff to an acceptable shiver. On most yachts when sailing on a close reach, the sheet is used for the course adjustment of the sail and the traveller is used for the fine tune.

As the wind becomes broader, you will be able to utilise more power and so the sail should be made fuller by straightening the mast, and easing the clew outhaul; the draft will then move forward necessitating a reduction in luff tension.

In waves, the helmsman will be working the boat up and down to maintain the best speed and the mainsail will need to be trimmed constantly to keep it at its optimum efficiency. Once the spinnaker is set, broaching could become a problem, especially in gusty conditions and the mainsail trimmer must work in concert with the helmsman to prevent broaches. The mainsail creates most of the force that tries to turn the boat into the wind and it is therefore the sail that should be eased first. If the helm is having control difficulties, let the sheet go first and if that is not sufficient knock off the kicking strap to release the leech and allow the sail to twist right off and spill wind. Once control has been regained, gently get the vang back on and sheet in – not too fast or control could be lost again.

Mainsail Trimming on a Run

On a run or a very broad reach, the mainsail is no longer capable of being trimmed as an aerofoil. Here the sail will be permanently stalled no matter what you do, but it still needs trimming. Use the kicking strap to get the top batten just about in line with the boom (when looking from below) and ease the sheet out as far as it will go without the sail flapping. Do not be concerned if it rests against the shrouds so long as there are anti-chafe patches on the sail for the spreader ends.

When running square in this way, shape is not too important and sail area counts for more, so have the clew outhaul and the halyard trimmed so that the clew and head are at their respective black bands, but do not overdo it and put stretch creases in the sail. (If creases appear ease the clew outhaul and/or the halyard only just sufficiently to remove them.)

Photo 2.18 Here the trimmer is playing the fine-tune sheet and the traveller simultaneously. The fine-tune, as its name implies, is good for small adjustments but when larger sheet movements are required the main sheet proper would be close to the trimmer's hand. It lies through the ratchet block on the cockpit floor just ahead of the traveller.

When running in really windy conditions, a rhythmic roll might be set up which is both uncomfortable and slow. One of the reasons for this oscillation is having too slack a leech on the mainsail. In a gust the top of the sail will twists forward of the mast and induces a weather roll and in the lulls the sail shrinks back such that the top of the sail is heeling the boat to leeward. The cure is to either sheet in a little or tighten the kicking strap to prevent the head twisting off excessively.

Mainsail – Gybing

Sometime it is possible to let the boom crash from side to side during a gybe but normally the mainsail should be brought at least part of the way towards the centreline of the boat. Remember that while the mainsail is in the near amidships, the boat will be harder to control and so you must be prepared to let the sail out again as soon as possible. Experiment with different positions within the cockpit to find the most efficient and comfortable place to be located throughout the gybe. Elbow-room will be certainly be required to sheet in and in heavy weather or on larger yachts do not be afraid to ask for a second person to help.

Work hard, look at the sail constantly and discuss the requirements with both the helmsman and the genoa trimmers. The job of a mainsail trimmer is not too difficult – but certainly strenuous.

Sweeper/General Crew

On any yacht with more than two crew, there is always the need for a general hand to fill in all the odd jobs which are not quite covered by the others. On larger yachts, there may well be more than one such person; on smaller yachts, specific crew members may have to pick up these extra tasks in addition to the core activity of their crew position.

This is the sort of role which is probably best suited to the younger members of the crew, those who are not yet too proud to go and pack a sail or tidy up. This does not mean that the job can be done by anyone who is too inexperienced, far from it, but keenness and the ability to spot when a job needs doing are more important than any specialised skill.

Because the job is by definition fairly non-specific, this member of the crew needs to be flexible and should be able to fill in wherever needed. Helping on the bow for sail changes, trimming the pole up and down while sailing downwind, packing the spinnaker after a drop and so on.

Little praise will tend to come the way of this crew member either – the trimmers or helmsman get that when the yacht is ahead – but nonetheless his or her role is still important to the overall smooth running of any manoeuvre and it takes a motivated person to fulfil this kind of role well.

It can be a good way to improve your own sailing. Being less tied to one place on the boat, you will be able to see how each expert works and also see the problems associated with each specific task.

Photo 2.19→Fighting a tangled, wet piece of slippery nylon below decks on a bumpy beat demands a strong stomach. Learning to pack a spinnaker quickly and with the certainty that nothing is twisted is an important part of the sweeper's role.

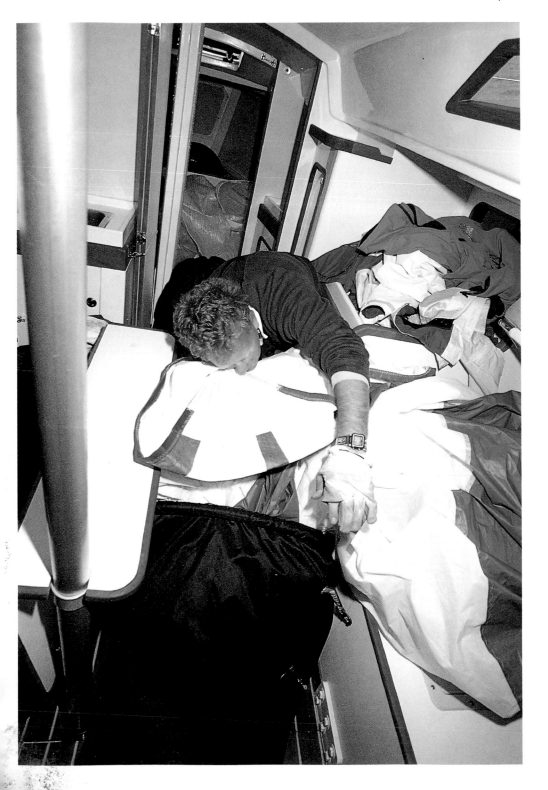

Bowman's Assistant/Sweeper

This is one of the key areas on larger yachts. Especially when making sail changes, it will be necessary for someone to assist the bowman with the preparation of the new sail and with dropping and subsequently packing the old one. This may well entail going below to get the new sail, so the sweeper should not be too prone to seasickness. Packing sails below is another sweaty task which sets many a stomach heaving.

On larger yachts he will probably set up the spinnaker pole for the hoist while the bowman is preparing the spinnaker. In a gybe set he may well top the pole as soon as the genoa is across and out of the way. In a simple bear away set his role may be to help with grinding the guy back – or in lighter airs there may not be a job for him to do except to get his weight in the 'right' place and keep his eyes open in case anyone needs help.

In a headsail change, the new sail must be found and got onto deck as quickly as possible. The halyard must be sorted, making sure that it is not twisted or snagged, the sheet leads will need repositioning for the new sail and the sheets themselves need to be re-led and attached to the new clew. Once the sail is on the bow, the sailbag needs throwing below, the halyard will need sweating up and then the old sail will be dropped. Finally the old sail will be dragged off the foredeck as quickly as possible and re-packed, either on the windward side-deck or possibly down below. The sweeper needs to be able to help with any of these jobs as required – the bowman will do some, the trimmers some and the pitman some – but there are normally at least one or two loose ends which are not covered by anyone else.

If packing the old headsail on deck, it is normally most important to get the weight of the sail and crew members off the bow as the first priority (except possibly in very light winds and smooth waters). The foot of the sail will need to be stretched out as far as possible, nearly always with the luff towards the bow and then the sail will be flaked as neatly as possible. Remember that this is not a 'harbour stow' and so long as the sail fits into the sausage bag, does not have any twists and has the whole luff tied with a sail-tie at the front of the bag – nothing else is necessary. When teaching this sort of flaking, I encourage the person working at the luff to start with one or two flakes and then the person working up the leech to follow, flaking independently and roughly pulling out the creases in the sail as he goes. In nearly all cases, the zipper should end up at the front of the bag and should have been prepared so that it can be slipped right off at one side prior to the next hoist so that the bag will split open when required.

Tacking

When tacking, the non-specific tasks are:

1. To help the genoa around the shrouds and make sure that it does not catch on the spreaders

2. To ensure that the old sheet runs free and, on larger boats of above thirty-eight feet, to grab the clew of the sail and fall back with it to help it in on the new tack.

There may be other jobs as well, such as pulling the tacking line (attached half way along the foot of the sail) to drag the clew forward of a babystay, or even removing and replacing the babystay during tacks in some circumstances. Once again, if the conditions or yacht size do not require any of these activities, then this crew member must still ensure his weight is in the best place at all times. In light winds, and especially on lightweight yachts, it is important to roll tack the yacht as far as is possible. This means keeping her heeled to leeward until the sails start to cross the centreline and then moving really quickly to the new leeward side and leaning out hard,

Photo 2.20 Generally helping the bowman on the foredeck is an essential task for the sweeper.

either on the guard-rails or on the shrouds until the yacht is settled on the new tack when the crew weight needs to be (gently) put forward and to leeward.

Gybe

In a gybe, it will depend very much on those jobs not covered by other crew. Maybe the mainsheet trimmer will need help in sweating the sheet, the new guy may need to be wound back in a hurry or perhaps the pole lift could need tailing up when the bowman has put the new guy into the pole jaws. If the boat has a fractional rig with running backstays, one of them may need to be released or tightened in heavy weather – in light airs it is normal for just one person to manage both runners.

Once the spinnaker has been dropped, either at the leeward mark or during a peel, the old sail will need to be repacked. This is one of the jobs which will almost certainly fall to the sweeper. If packing on a boat that is new to you, ensure that you have helped with the packing before the race began so that you will know how the crew like the sails prepared – are elastic bands or wool used as stopping? – for example. If the spinnaker has just been dropped at the leeward mark, do not go below immediately to repack it, wait until everything has settled down and the yacht is up to speed, then ask if 'now' is a good time before disappearing below.

Weight and Position

Most modern racing yachts are sensitive to the distribution of crew weight and the lighter the yacht, the more this will become true. You, along with the rest of the crew must always think about where your weight will do most good and then endeavour to be in that position for as much time as possible. If you need to do a job which takes you away from this ideal place, do it as quickly and efficiently as you can and then get back to where your weight will help most.

On the wind, the adopted position should be with legs out over the side, head under the top guard-rail and with the lower rail pressed hard into the ribs. It is also important to sense the heel of the boat, if one person is off the rail for a short time make an extra effort to sit out

hard. When there is a short lull in the wind and the yacht comes upright, be ready to sit in or even move to leeward. In very light conditions, especially when there are waves or swell, it is unusual for the yacht to require the entire crew to sail her. In these circumstances, your weight is probably best down below, to leeward and forward where it will reduce the pitching moments to a minimum.

Downwind, think about how far fore or aft you should be and do not be afraid to ask if you are not sure. On a screaming run in half a gale it may be necessary for the whole crew to get as far back as possible, but as soon as the helmsman has full and easy control of the boat it will normally pay to move the weight a little forward and as the wind drops still more, so should the crew continue to shift further forward.

Tidying

This does not mean sweeping and polishing, but sorting out the snake-pit that develops in every cockpit after a manoeuvre. Possibly assistance may be required in sorting out the sheets and guys after a spinnaker drop. Get to know which rope does what and how the individual crew members who use them like them to be tidied. Some lines may go down the main hatch, others may be put through small cockpit windows and some will be flaked into bags. The genoa sheets in particular and any other lines which may need to be let fly in a hurry (halyards, spinnaker guys etc.) should not be coiled or else they are likely to get knotted as they fly out. Ropes like these should always be flaked in loose figure of eights and the kinks need to be worked out of the free ends of the ropes. When sitting in the cockpit with nothing else to do, look at which ropes are getting out of control and have a quick tidy up.

To reiterate, the good general crew can help with most jobs on the yacht even though he may not be an expert at any of them. Keep your eyes open, be ready to accept advice from those who have more experience and be

Photo 2.21 Whenever the opportunity arises, ropes should be sorted and tidied. If something can go wrong with a length of line – it generally will.

prepared to at least listen to those who have actually got less experience than you, but are either older or more 'senior' than you on the boat and you will progress quickly.

The Helmsman

The person steering the boat is often considered to be the most important member of the crew. In my opinion, although it is clearly an important position, most aspects of the job can be learnt quite quickly by someone with the right aptitude. This leads to the possibility that other more experienced crew members can do other jobs, which I consider to be equally if not more demanding, such as tactics.

One of the most frequent problems that I see while coaching or regatta sailing is the helmsman who also tries to be the tactician, the person in charge of sail trim and just about every other important function that it takes to run a boat. Obviously the person steering must have a feel for the tactical situation and in some circumstances there might not be anyone else with the necessary experience to take on the role of tactician, but on a well crewed boat, the helmsman should concentrate on steering, almost to the exclusion of anything else.

I have had the pleasure of sailing with many top class helms and all are different in their approach. There are however some areas that are common to most. The skills can be learned, but there are certain attitudes and attributes that can enable progress from a reasonable club level helm to someone who is able to cope with top class competition.

Concentration is the most obvious of these attributes, especially when sailing in flat water. Of all those with whom I have sailed, Rodney Pattisson (Olympic Gold medallist) is perhaps the most extreme. He locks himself into the position, gets into the 'groove' and can then keep the boat (almost any boat) going within point one of a knot of optimum speed for hours on end. His vast dinghy sailing experience has also imbided him with the facility to be aware of what is going on around him without losing concentration. Not the most communicative of helmsmen while steering, but wonderful to watch.

Another equally important attribute of the good helm is a feel for the boat. To acquire an almost innate ability to sense how she will accelerate, turn or handle in waves takes years of practice. I was fortunate to sail with Mauro Pelaschier and he is a helmsman who has this ability. His background is in the Olympic classes plus two *America*'s Cup campaigns, and this in addition to the 'normal' run of international regattas sailed in many sizes of boat gives him a huge variety of experiences from which to draw whenever he steps onto a new boat. After just one day of practise, he was able to get a Swan 53 to target speeds within seconds, to feel whether a tack was fast or not,

Photo 2.22 The helmsman's steering position should be comfortable, with a good back support (Some plastic tube or padding on the guard-rail helps considerably.) and with something to brace his feet against. He should have a clear view of the headsail tell-tales, the instruments and the approaching waves.

even without the data from the Deckman computer and could also handle her through gybes in thirty plus knots of wind as if he had steered her all his life.

Lawrie Smith is another World class helm with whom I have had the pleasure to sail. His main talent seems to be in managing to get the absolute maximum speed out of the yacht at all times, steering downwind with a flair and feel that is unusual even at his level. Much more flamboyant in style than Rodney, they made an invincible pair when they were sailing together on the one-tonner *Jamarella*, with Rodney steering most of the time upwind and Lawrie taking over for downwind legs. They also shared the tactics as well, thus allowing each other to concentrate fully on helming.

All good helms need to have the skills exhibited by the three names I have mentioned here; these particular people are notable because they each have a very different style and each is quite extreme in his particular talent.

Steering at the Start

When starting it is most important for the helmsman to have a feel for the acceleration capability of the boat being steered. Spatial awareness of distance from the line and in relation to the other boats around is also an important attribute. To start successfully requires a fair measure of aggression tempered by safety. You should also be able to trust your tactician and bowman implicitly.

On a crowded line, it is rare for there to be sufficient time for the tactician to call the shots and the helmsman must be able to make his own decisions on a second by second basis. (Not true of match racing). Knowing whether to slow down for a gap at the last moment or to accelerate through to the next gap often needs to be decided virtually instantaneously. On the final approach to the line, with the bowman calling distance to go in boat lengths, an acute awareness of the speed of the yacht becomes vital.

You should also be aware of your own limitations. There is little point in attempting a perfect start at the favoured end of the line when you are not confident of your ability to pull it off. It may be prudent to give away just a little in order to ensure a good but nevertheless safe start.

Steering Upwind in Flat Water

When steering in flat water it is important to concentrate on the combination of wind angle and boat speed. Use the luff tell-tales on the genoa as the steering guide but remember to tell the genoa trimmer what you are trying to achieve. If the boat feels slow or is actually slow (measured against a competitor or known optimum boat speed) then get the trimmer to ease sheets slightly. Similarly, if a patch of rougher water needs to be negotiated, more power will be needed and again the trimmer should be asked to ease. Generally, if the water is smooth and the wind fairly steady, it should

be possible to get into the groove quite easily.

If the boat's performance has been accurately calibrated and recorded, the use of target speeds can be helpful. In fact, even if the boat is relatively unknown to you it is sensible to ascertain the speed when she feels right and then keep within small limits of that speed – so long as the wind stays constant in strength. Always use targets with caution however, even if the instruments are well calibrated, all sorts of factors can influence the optimum compromise between speed and angle; wind sheer, how hard the crew are sitting out, the exact sea conditions and so on. If you are using targets, remember that they are the optimum speed and not a speed to be exceeded. If you are sailing faster than your target it probably indicates that your wind angle is too large and the resulting VMG (velocity made good) will be less than optimum.

Never steer to maximise your VMG! If you attempt this you will end up chasing the VMG up and down like a yo-yo. This is because of the inertia inherent in any yacht which delays her response to your steering. Get the trimmers to play with the trim to maximise VMG over a period of around thirty seconds and then settle on that angle and speed as your target for that wind strength.

Tacking in smooth water can be carried out fairly rapidly. Certainly the turn towards the wind can be quite fast, unless the wind speed is very low. After a tack it should be possible to bear away accurately to a heading a degree or so broader than is normal, allow the speed to pick up to within a tenth of a knot of target and then harden up to the usual windward angle. (Try hard not to sail too low when accelerating as this will lose a lot of windward ground to no purpose.) When using a big genoa near the top of its wind range, slow the second half of the tack to give the winch grinders time to sheet the sail in.

Fig 2.17
Polar Diagram

This example shows the potential maximum performance of a yacht sailing in a True Wind of ten knots.

It will have been created by either the builder and designer, or by the crew. For the serious racing yacht it is an important piece of information and is shown here in simple form. The data collection will have involved many hours of sailing and recording and charts will have been created for many different wind strengths.

It is usual to add other information to each diagram that will show the sail combinations that were used to achieve the figures shown, thereby indicating that critical change between a two-sail reach and when best to hoist the spinnaker. Much of this information can be loaded into an onboard computer to predict a mass of sailing and navigational information.

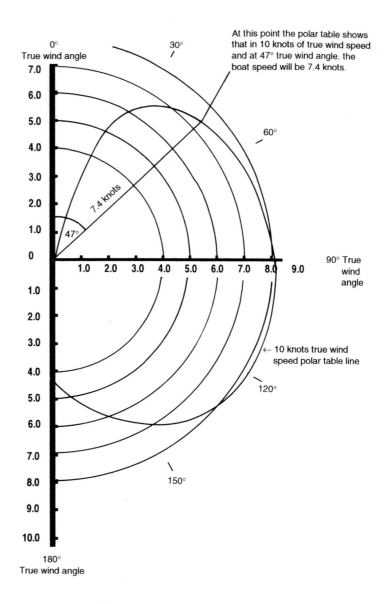

At this point the polar table shows that in 10 knots of true wind speed and at 47° true wind angle. the boat speed will be 7.4 knots.

← 10 knots true wind speed polar table line

Steering Upwind in Waves

Here it will be hard to get into a real target speed groove and it is vital that you develop a feel for the wave pattern. This means that you must be sitting (or standing if using a wheel) where you can see the next couple of waves approaching. Get one of the crew on the weather rail to call particularly big waves as they approach, especially at night.

The technique used most often is to steer the boat so that it points higher up the face of the wave and then bear away down its back. This is good because the apparent wind moves aft as the bow pitches up and forward again as the bow goes down. Therefore altering the angle to the waves helps to keep the sails give maximum power at all times. Although this sounds easy, in practice it is a technique which takes some getting used to. The problem is to anticipate what is going to be required a second or two before it is needed and apply the appropriate helm movements before the boat needs to turn. To merely wait until the bottom of the trough before applying helm to point up an approaching wave face will inevitably result in the boat responding at the crest and vice versa. This ends up with you being totally out of phase and slower than if you had kept the helm straight.

Tacking in waves should not be a problem. If possible wait for a flat patch before starting to tack and make sure that you have good speed before commencing the turn. If there are no flat bits of water around, try to turn so that the bow is not stopped halfway through by a wave crest.

Target speeds can still be used, even in rough water, but you need to have a greater tolerance in your idea of the targets. One definite no-no is to attempt to point too high. This will always end up with the boat being slowed appreciably by slamming into the waves. Make sure that the trimmers are setting the sails for a couple of degrees lower than your flat water angles.

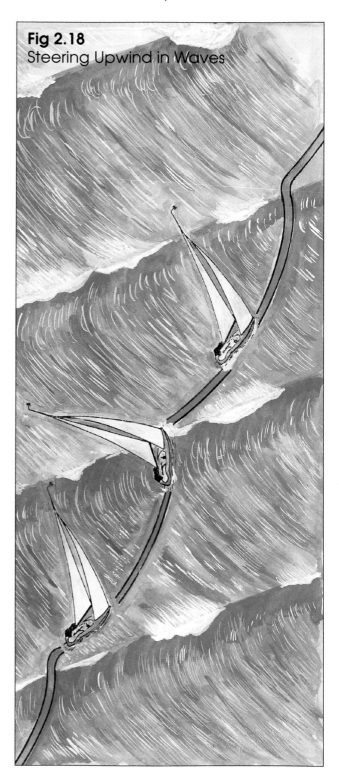

Fig 2.18
Steering Upwind in Waves

Steering Upwind in Gusty Conditions

In heavy gusting conditions yet another technique is needed. The boat will usually be set up to have the right sail combination for the average wind strength and will be overpowered when the gusts hit and lacking power in the worst of the lulls. The way to cope with a wildly unsteady wind strength is to feather the boat through the gusts. Do not attempt to steer a straight course, as that would result in excessive heel which then creates too much

leeway. The genoa trimmer should sheet in really hard during the gusts and the mainsheet trimmer should simultaneously ease the traveller down its track. When you feel the boat coming upright in a lull, bear away slightly; the genoa should be eased at the same time and the traveller pulled more to windward. If possible, the backstay should be eased a little.

Try to get an idea of directional wind changes in the gusts. In the northern hemisphere gusts will often veer (opposite in the southern hemisphere), giving a freer on starboard tack and a corresponding header on port. Get a crew member to call changes in wind strength.

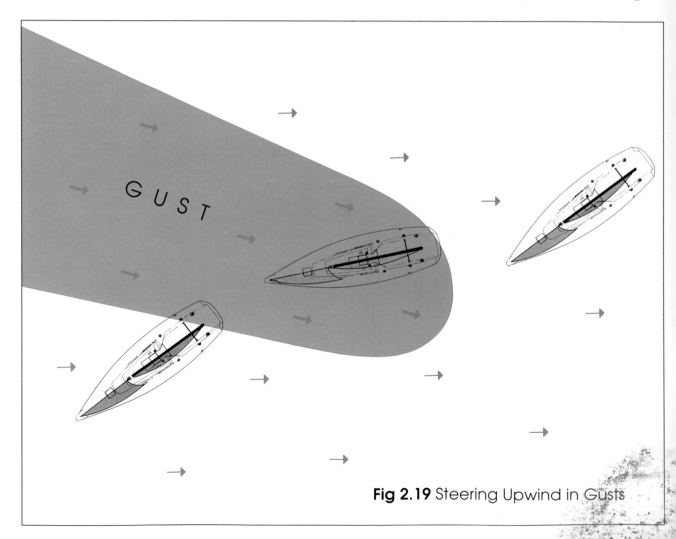

Fig 2.19 Steering Upwind in Gusts

Steering on a Reach

The general principle of steering on a reach is to keep the boat racing at maximum speed and at the same time maintaining the required course. Unless conditions are fair and consistent, do not try to keep on an exact compass course; play the waves and gusts/lulls to get the best speed and a good average course.

Depending on the angle of waves to your required compass course, it may or may not be possible to make use of them for surfing. Experiment a little, trying a few degrees both high and low of the course to see if it is possible to gain. Do ensure that the navigator knows what you are doing as there is little point in going half a knot faster but thirty degrees off course.

Steering to Get a Tow

When handicap racing, it is frequent for some boats to get to the weather mark ahead of others who will then be faster on the reach. In this situation on a boat that is not so hot on a reach, it may be worthwhile attempting to get a tow on the stern wave of the faster boats as they come past. Your tactician should be deciding if this is a sensible option. If the helmsman spends his time looking around to judge whether a particular boat is going to give an advantageous tow he will probably be going off course.

The basics of getting a tow are as follows

1. Get as close to the stern of the larger boat as possible, ideally in her primary stern wave

2. Do not sit on her wind once you are on the tow.

3. Make her go to leeward if possible as she overtakes, but do not slow her too much unless she is considerably faster than you. This could mean deliberately steering high to allow her to pass several boat lengths to leeward and then bearing away once she is through you dirty air.

4. Work really hard to keep in her stern wave. Do not become overpowered and broach as her wave picks you up. Steer the boat as if it was a large surf-board once you are riding her wave.

In order to achieve all this, it is vital that both the trimmers and tactician understand exactly what you are doing. Once you get on her wave it is too late to start explanations!

Steering on a Reach in Gusty Conditions

The gust must be anticipated before it hits otherwise the boat will simply heel excessively and not accelerate; it may even broach. A crew member should be looking to windward to search for the signs of an approaching gust on the water's surface or by watching other boats.

As a gust approaches the helmsman should bear away slightly (as the trimmers ease the sails to maintain optimum power without heel) and then, as the yacht accelerates in the gust you can gently, ever so gently, come back up to course. The reverse is true in lulls. Here, you will need to luff slightly in order to keep good speed during the lull.

Even if you steer straight during the gusts, the trimmers will need to ease the sheets as the gust hits because the apparent wind will move aft.

Fig 2.20 A Tow on a Stern Wave

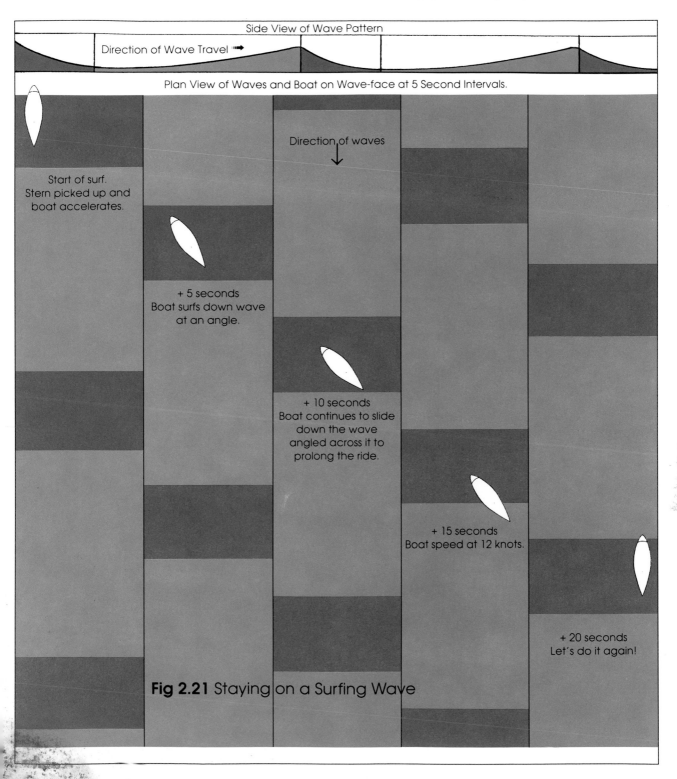

Side View of Wave Pattern

Direction of Wave Travel ➡

Plan View of Waves and Boat on Wave-face at 5 Second Intervals.

Start of surf.
Stern picked up and
boat accelerates.

Direction of waves
↓

+ 5 seconds
Boat surfs down wave
at an angle.

+ 10 seconds
Boat continues to slide
down the wave
angled across it to
prolong the ride.

+ 15 seconds
Boat speed at 12 knots.

+ 20 seconds
Let's do it again!

Fig 2.21 Staying on a Surfing Wave

Steering Downwind

On a run we are again using VMG (for the trimmers) and target speeds and angles for the helm.

In light airs the most important person is the spinnaker trimmer. He is the one who can feel whether you have enough pressure in the sail to be able to sail squarer to the wind or if the pressure has dropped making it necessary to luff up for speed. This means that it is crucial to have a good working relationship between the trimmer and the helm, they must work together as a team at all times.

Generally you will be trying to sail as low as possible while maintaining reasonable speed. This will always be a compromise and will change with both wind speed and wave conditions.

Make use of the crew weight to keep the balance feeling right. Heeling to windward can often be faster in lightish airs because it places the centre of effort of the sails above the keel and therefore reduces the need for rudder movement to keep the boat going in a straight line. Whenever you have control problems in stronger winds, keep the boat heeled slightly to leeward as this will help to prevent a leeward broach.

Steering to Surf

Good helming technique can make a huge difference to average boat speed in marginal surfing conditions. When a boat surfs down a wave its speed can easily increase by up to forty or even fifty per cent and it is therefore crucial to keep surfing for as long as possible. As a wave picks up the stern, bear away (probably quite sharply) to aim virtually straight down the face of the wave; this will point the boat downhill and help to initiate the surf. Once surfing, attempt to extend the ride to gain the maximum period of dramatically increased speed. As with a surfer on a Malibu board, this can often be achieved by steering a little across the face of the wave to extend the time before you hit the trough.

When bearing away initially, the trimmers should ease the sheets, then as the yacht accelerates down the wave and the apparent wind moves forward, the sheets can be trimmed in again. As with most other points of sailing, the helm and trimmers must work as a team for surfing to be a success.

(See Fig 2.21)

Steering Through a Gybe

In my view the helmsman is by far the most important crew member while gybing. The bowman is often blamed for being too slow when a spinnaker gybe goes wrong, but a good helm should be able to steer through the gybe and keep the sail full however long it takes.

In anything other than very light air gybes, where the yacht must turn from reach to reach in one continuous and uninterrupted movement, the principles of steering through a gybe are as follows

1. Say 'Stand by to gybe' – the crew get ready.

2. Say 'Bearing away' – the mainsheet comes in as the boat bears away to a dead run; just before square running call 'trip'.

3. The crew trip the pole away, the trimmer keeps the spinnaker under control with the sheets and the helm steers to keep the sail filled and to stop it lurching out of control. Do not complete the gybe at this stage.

4. When the new guy is in the pole and the pole is squared back, complete the turn smoothly and gybe the mainsail.

The critical points are to maintain control when the guy is tripped away from the pole and the spinnaker is allowed to fly free; to steer almost (but not quite) dead downwind while the spinnaker is free and not get swung round onto a reach (and broach) by the waves; to complete the gybe only after the spinnaker has been gybed.

The Helmsman – Conclusion

There are other aspects of steering which we have not covered in this chapter but hopefully the areas we have considered will assist you to improve your technique. To improve further -

a) Spend as long as possible steering on the water. It does not matter on what type of boat, the more variety the better in the long term. A fair proportion of this practice should be in a competitive environment.

b) Sail with people who are better helmsmen than yourself; watch them, talk to them and copy their good points.

The Team as a Whole

In this chapter we have so far considered each crew position individually. This final piece looks at how to put the entire crew together so that they work as a team. Without this unity the crew will remain a bunch of individuals and the boat will not achieve its full potential.

Understanding Each Other

There are many facets of working as a team. One of the most important is that each member must respect the strengths of the others and understand any weaknesses.

To become a winning crew you should sail together frequently so that you get to know each other quite well. It may be that a world class bowman can perform an outside headsail change (or whatever) in a Force Seven, with no help and in less than thirty seconds, but if your bowman takes three minutes to do the same thing, then, for the time being at least, you must all accept that fact. Top helmsmen may always be able to achieve a good start, but

if your helmsman is wary of mixing it too closely on a crowded start-line in a breeze with the result that you normally only make a mediocre start, so be it. They will get better with practice and there is no point in any of the crew getting upset and thus adding pressure unnecessarily to people who are undoubtedly trying their hardest.

In most situations it helps for the crew to socialise together off the boat as well as racing together. In this way you get to know each other much better and can discuss problems without the pressure of a racing environment. Debriefing sessions after a race can also add to this process. These need to be open and informal so that even the least experienced and most junior members of the crew feel able to have their say – without being put down by those with more experience.

One yacht on which I have done a lot of racing is the Swan 53. Here we always have a debriefing after every race or training session. I generally start the ball rolling with a brief outline of the race and one or two important points which have emerged during the day. Every crew member in turn – not in any particular order – then has the opportunity to add his or her piece, either about how he performed, about any of the rest of the crew or indeed about any part of the yacht and its equipment that effects his job. In this way, any gripes or worries are brought into the open and dealt with as appropriate. When everyone else has had a turn, I summarise the salient points, the owner adds his views as to how the day went and we make a job list, decide on changes and any further training that is necessary and we go on to do better in the next race.

Have a Common Goal

During the coaching that I do on many boats, one of the most common problems that I find is the lack of a common goal. The whole crew must know and agree with the aims of a particular session; this may be a race, a training sail or an instrument calibration session.

If actually racing, an achievable goal needs to be set. For example, if you normally come two thirds of the way down a fleet it is not entirely rational to expect to win. Maybe you will, but if you go out and become disappointed when you finish half way down the fleet, your sights were set too high. In this case you should all be pleased to have improved on your average performance and not be upset because you did not win. This does not mean that you shouldn't go out and try to win every race, far from it, but be realistic about what is achievable.

When entering for a series of races then the same principles need to be applied. You need to decide as a crew what are the aims of the series or regatta. Some regattas may be sailed with only part of the normal crew, plus wives, friends and so on, in the knowledge that the results are unlikely to be as good as could normally be expected. This is no problem so long as everyone is aware of the situation, but it would cause tension if some of the regular crew had not been briefed clearly. Another regatta may see the addition of one or more specialised crew members to strengthen the normal team. Once again, no problem so long as the crew changes are handled sensibly and the reasons given to any of the regulars for leaving them off or changing their roles on the yacht.

When undertaking training or instrument calibration sessions, try to be realistic about which of the crew are going to benefit from a planned session and, especially in the latter case, do not have too many of the crew aboard simply because you are going out sailing. Calibrating the log might only need three people, while calibrating the true wind direction will probably need another couple, but it is unlikely to give satisfaction to the entire crew. Few things turn crew members off a campaign more than being required to attend sessions, only to find that they were not needed in the first place. Most crews will have family or other calls on their time in addition to

racing (unless they are paid professionals) and this should be borne in mind in the planning.

First Do Your Own Job Properly

On some boats, various crew members either try to help with other people's jobs or, much worse, criticise other crew members when their own tasks are not being done properly.

Constructive criticism is nearly always helpful but must be done diplomatically and not while a stressful task is actually being performed. For example, the time to tell the bowman that there is an easier way to do an outside genoa change is not while he is up to his armpits in sea-water with the sail half up; before starting the manoeuvre might be ideal but afterwards, in a debriefing mode, is definitely better than shouting at the hapless chap who is struggling enough to complete the task. Helping other members of the crew to better fulfil their role is also helpful but must not be at the expense of another function in the same manoeuvre.

Training

In order to improve your overall performance it is important to train together. Once again this allows problems to be sorted without the stresses brought about by racing.

When going out for a training session, the aims must be clearly defined. If the conditions change so that these aims become difficult or impossible to achieve, then change your plans – and ensure that every member of the crew knows what is happening.

Training can be even more intense than racing and too much should not be done in too short a time. Short intense sessions of half to one hour, followed by a break and a debrief are much more productive than a single two to three hour session with no breaks. In the latter case, some members of the crew will become tired and most people lose concentration after forty five minutes of work. The sessions should be arranged so that everyone is involved, rather than having one or two crew working really hard with the rest sitting around doing nothing.

If you are going to try a new manoeuvre, fully brief the crew before you start and discuss the various aspects of the manoeuvre which may cause individuals a problem.

One potentially powerful way to assist in the melding of a team is to employ a professional coach for one or two training sessions. Even if you all feel that your crew work is going adequately well, an outside person coming on board and watching how the team performs can reap enormous benefits. It is not necessarily that the coach has any more experience than other individuals on the boat, more that it is much easier to accept constructive criticism from an outsider than from someone within a team. If hard decisions are required about crew positions, the coach can come along, make his recommendations and then leave. The team will still be working together and there will be no bitterness or feelings of having been 'got at' among the crew.

Communicate

Another chief area of potential complaint is when there is a lack of communication among the crew. The importance of good communication cannot be overstressed and pervades all aspects of getting the best out of the boat and crew.

Arrival times for a race, what gear is needed and/or allowed to be brought by the crew, what commitment is really expected in terms of time outside the racing programme itself are all obvious examples of where the skipper must ensure that the whole crew understand how the boat is being run. While sailing, communication between the individual crew members is of paramount importance. The bowman must be able to let the helm know how far the boat is from the line on the approach to the start and there must be a

system for the bowman to indicate overlap situations at the start and when rounding marks. The helm must let the trimmers know what he is trying to achieve in any given situation and they must reciprocate by letting the helm know, for example, if he is sailing too high or low for optimum Vmg (velocity made good). The navigator should not only calculate the course to steer and distance/bearing to the next mark, but he must also communicate the options available and his view on the consequences of each of these. And so on and so on!

Summary

Any crew is made up of a number of individuals. For them to work effectively together they must work as a team and not as a bunch of prima-donnas. The skipper has a vital role in getting the crew to pull together and must nip any griping or whinging firmly in the bud. Common aims and achievable goals are essential and there needs to be at least a core of regulars who are capable of racing the yacht to the agreed level.

Sailing with a good team, with everyone knowing their job, and having practised enough to be able to cope with any situation without worry is a wonderful thing – especially in a wild gybe broach in heavy seas in the middle of the night when it is nice to know your fellow sailors quite well. On the other hand, sailing with a bunch of people who have different aims, have little or no respect for each other and who criticise the other crew members behind their backs is a recipe for general unhappiness. Given the choice between sailing with a team of relative beginners who enjoy their sailing and who understand their limitations and sailing with a crew made up of the 'experts' for each role, but who distrust each other and are incapable of sailing as a team, I would always go for the former. After all, sailing is meant to be fun!

Chapter 3
Sail Trim

Sail trimming is akin to tuning the engine on a racing car. Unless the sails are being trimmed properly at all times, you will lose power and therefore the boat speed will drop. It is vital that except in very steady conditions, the sails are trimmed continuously and not cleated off as they might be on a cruiser.

It is important to understand the various sail controls which the trimmers have to play with and adjust and each section will deal with the relevant controls as they apply to that point of sailing.

Headsails

The first control to consider is probably the halyard. This works on the luff of the sail, stretching it tighter as more load is applied. As the luff is stretched, so 'spare' cloth is drawn from the middle of the sail towards the front thus moving the draft in the sail forward. This will tend to make the front of the sail more rounded and conversely will give a straighter leech. In most cases the halyard tension should be adjusted to put the point of maximum draft about forty to forty-five per cent of the way from luff to leech.
(See Illustration 2.7)

Next let's look at the tension of the forestay. This is not always easily adjustable while sailing but is an important control. Because genoas are normally used when going upwind or close reaching, the centre of the forestay will always be blown back towards the sail. This in turn allows the front of the sail itself to move towards the middle of the sail and as can be seen, the more this happens the fuller the middle of the sail will become. This means that if we want to flatten the sail (to depower it in stronger winds) then we must tighten the forestay to straighten it, whereas if we need a fuller genoa then we can afford to have a slacker forestay.

(See Illustration 2.9)

The fore and aft position of the genoa sheet lead is next on the agenda. This controls the relative tensions applied to the leech and the foot of the genoa as it is sheeted in. On old cross cut sails with a mitre seam running from the clew to the luff, it was normal to adjust the fore and aft position of the sheet lead so that the sheet pulled straight along the line of the mitre seam. Nowadays, most genoas are either cut with horizontal panels or vertical cut, with all the panels running up and down the sail and more normally on racing sails, designed with a complex mix of panels to optimise the stress loadings within the sail. None of these sails has a mitre seam to give us our guide as to the correct position of the sheet, although some sails will have an arrow marked near the clew to give us an idea of the correct angle.

What we really want to do with the fore and aft sheet position is to ensure that the whole sail is working and that there is the right amount of twist to compensate for differences in apparent wind angle on differing parts of the sail. The way to see this is to have tell-tales on the luff of the sail, one set about a quarter of the way up, another halfway and a final set three quarters of the way towards the head. With the sheet in, the yacht can be luffed gently towards the wind, and the reaction on all three sets of tell-tales noted. Ideally, in moderate conditions, all should respond at the same time. If, as will often happen, the top tell-tales break before the centre ones, then the sheet lead is too far aft, allowing the leech of the sail to twist to leeward too much and thus losing power out of the head of the sail. If on the other hand the lowest tell-tales break first, then the top of the sail is over trimmed, the leech is too tight and the sheet lead needs to be moved further aft.

(See Fig 2.10)

When using a sail which is too large for the immediate conditions, such as during a short-lived squall when you do not want to change down, it is useful to be able to lose power from the sail. This can be done by moving the sheet lead aft which deliberately allows the sail to twist off, thus losing power from the top and reducing the heeling forces.

A broadly similar setting of the sheet lead is required when sailing upwind in big waves. Here the apparent wind will be constantly changing as you pitch first up the wave and then down the other side. In this case it will not be possible to get all the tell-tales to fly correctly at all times and a compromise is needed. As the bow pitches down the wave,

this will increase the apparent wind on the sails and will also bring the apparent wind further forward. Conversely as the bow pitches up, the apparent wind will be drawn aft and will decrease slightly. Since we cannot get all the sail working for these varying wind angles, it makes most sense to move the sheet lead aft a little, thus allowing the top to twist off further than usual. This means that as the bow pitches forward down the wave and the wind increases, the top of the sail will flap, depowering as before, while as the bow pitches up and the wind comes aft and decreases, the top of the sail will work properly, giving more power just when it is required.

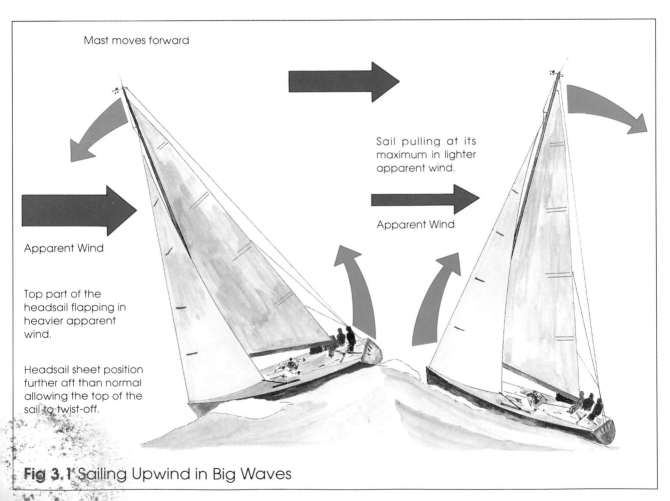

Mast moves forward

Sail pulling at its maximum in lighter apparent wind.

Apparent Wind

Apparent Wind

Top part of the headsail flapping in heavier apparent wind.

Headsail sheet position further aft than normal allowing the top of the sail to twist-off.

Fig 3.1 Sailing Upwind in Big Waves

Photo 3.2 Looking along the leeward side-deck there is a smallish headsail trimmed for beating to windward. The foot is sheeted so that the clew is pretty well in line with the lower shroud – this is a good reference for the trimmer.

Photo 3.1← Looking up the mast with a genoa set for windward work. Notice the spreaders which have been marked with reference points to gauge the distance of the sail from the spreader tip. Also the chafe patch where the sail will bear on the spreader when tacking.

The next control is the tension of the sheet itself. Since the helmsman will be sailing to make the luff tell-tales fly correctly, the trimmer is in control of the speed of the boat and of the angle sailed. The harder the sheet is pulled in, the closer the yacht will sail to the wind but the slower it will go, whereas easing the sheet will force the helmsman to sail lower and faster. Upwind it is all a compromise between speed and height and the crew need to know how fast the yacht should be going in a particular set of conditions – this can either be from performance data or from comparing your speed and height with other, similar boats around you. With an overlapping genoa that has been cut for the boat, it should be possible to trim the sail so that it just kisses the spreader ends with the foot hard against the base of the shrouds; this gives you the tightest possible setting. The spreader end should never be poking through the sail because this is not only slow, but is also likely to cause severe damage to the sail, especially during a tack. There should be communication going between the genoa trimmer and the helmsman as to what is required at any given time. If the helmsman needs to sail slightly low and fast, either to get through a choppy patch or to sail below another yacht, then the trimmer will need to ease the sheet slightly to allow this to happen. Similarly, if the helmsman needs to point high for a time, either because the sea is smooth and less power is needed or to keep above another yacht, then the sail will need to be trimmed harder than usual.(See Photos 3.1 & 3.2)

Upwind it can be very useful to have an instrument that displays VMG (velocity made good dead upwind) since maximising this readout will give the best compromise between speed and height. VMG is a trimmer's tool and not one for the helmsman otherwise all kinds of disasters will befall the boat speed. VMG will react immediately to changes of wind angle whereas the speed of the boat will lag some seconds behind due to inertia. This means that if the helmsman is trying to maximise VMG he will tend to get the boat sailing fast and the luff up. As he luffs, the VMG will increase, temporarily. Eventually the speed will drop and VMG will drop again, but by then the sails will be flapping and considerable ground will have been lost. It is best for the trimmer to watch VMG over a period of about thirty seconds. Once it has stabilised, he can then try trimming in a bit further and once again let VMG settle down to the new setting. If the average VMG is higher then once again he can try sheeting in a little harder. Eventually he will find the average VMG dropping and he then knows that he has overtrimmed the sail and should ease it back to the ideal setting.

Photo 3.3 Not every racing boat has the luxury of large-display instrument-repeaters such as these, but wherever such devices are positioned, they should be made visible to the helmsman and trimmers.

The final control over the shape of the genoa is the inboard sheeting position. In simple terms, the closer the sheeting position is to the centreline, the narrower will be the sheeting angle and the higher the boat will point. However, as the sheet lead is brought inboard, the slot between the genoa and the mainsail will also become narrower and this has good and bad points. In moderate airs, when the amount of air moving over the genoa is reasonable and the amount of power is not too great, it is an advantage to narrow the slot because this will increase the speed of air flow through the slot thus making both the genoa and mainsail work more efficiently. In very light airs you cannot have such a narrow slot since there will not be enough speed in the air flow to get it moving through a narrow slot. In these conditions it may still be correct to have a narrow sheeting angle because the sheet will also be eased, thus opening the slot again.

In heavy airs upwind, a wider sheeting angle will be required to allow the mainsail to be dropped down the track on the traveller or when reaching to allow the main to be eased considerably. Here, if the sheeting angle is too narrow, there will be excessive backwinding of the mainsail as soon as it is let down the track. Thus as you are either becoming overpowered with the combination of sails in use or need to reach off, it will become important to move the sheet lead further outboard. When reaching, moving the sheet-lead outboard will also help to keep the sail trimmed properly as the genoa sheet is eased.

In general, if you have the choice between an inner and outer genoa track, it will be best to use the inner one in light to moderate winds and to move the sheet to the outer one as you become overpowered. Once close reaching with the genoa, the sheet should be moved as far outboard as possible, probably to the toerail.

On a reach, the helmsman will more or less sail the required course and the trimmer should trim the sail to keep the tell-tales all working, easing the sheet if they stall and sheeting in if the windward ones flap.

Although it is theoretically possible for the trimmer to be constantly moving all his controls to achieve the optimum sail shape, it is rarely, if ever, feasible in practice. To start with, if the wind strength is changing very rapidly, it will not be possible to trim quickly enough and attempting to do so will probably end up with the sail always being wrong. Compromises need to be made, only adjusting the various sail controls for major changes in the wind. The other problem that usually gets in the way of continual trimming is the need to have the trimmer's weight on the side-deck. Once again a compromise is called for with the trimmer going to leeward to adjust the sail if a major change has occurred but otherwise setting the sail for the average conditions and then getting his weight out. Luckily it is usually in light airs that the maximum changes in wind speed will be found, at least on a percentage basis, and in these conditions it is obviously not so much of a problem to have weight to leeward.

Reaching is slightly different. Here the trimmer should be looking and adjusting constantly. He will be concentrating principally at the luff of the sail rather than at the whole sail shape and he should be able to do this from the windward side. Therefore unless on a big heavy boat, it is normally best to take the reaching sheet to the windward winch and trim from there.

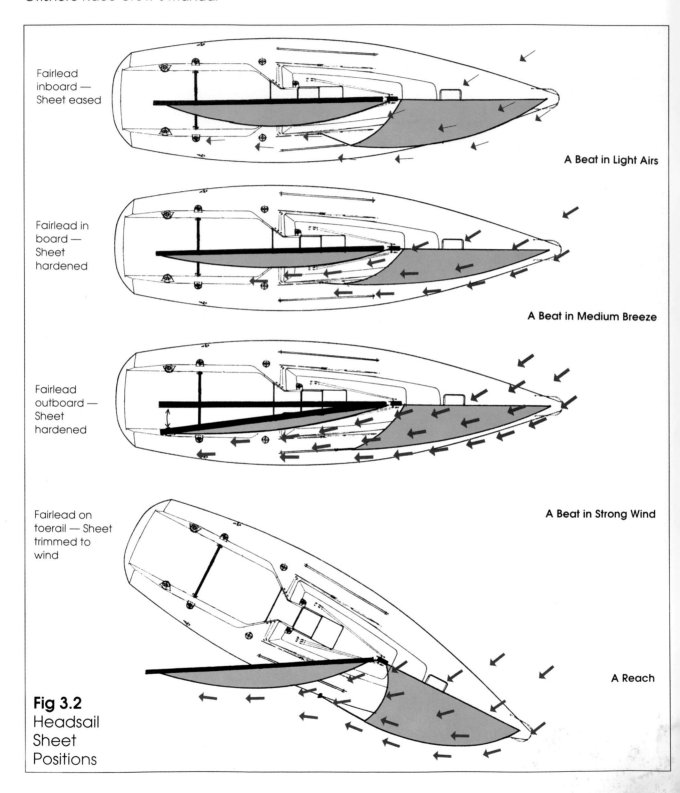

Fairlead
inboard —
Sheet eased

A Beat in Light Airs

Fairlead in
board —
Sheet
hardened

A Beat in Medium Breeze

Fairlead
outboard —
Sheet
hardened

A Beat in Strong Wind

Fairlead on
toerail — Sheet
trimmed to
wind

A Reach

Fig 3.2
Headsail
Sheet
Positions

Mainsail

The controls for the mainsail are fundamentally similar to those for the genoa but there are some differences.

The halyard controls the fore and aft position of the draft in the same way that it does on a genoa. Thus tightening the halyard will stretch the luff and bring the draft of the sail forward. We mentioned earlier that the optimum position for maximum draft in a genoa is about forty to forty five per cent back from the luff towards the leech. With the mainsail it should be slightly further aft because the front of the main cannot work effectively due to it's immediate proximity to the mast and also because the effect of the slot between the genoa and the main will tend to make it necessary to have a flatter entry. With most mainsails, the optimum draft position will be about half way between luff and leech, at least where there is an overlap. On a fractional rig boat the draft could be a little further forward near the top of the sail.

Under most rules, the mainsail will be limited in size by black bands on the mast at the tack and the head. In order to achieve maximum size in light airs the mainsail will be cut to utilize the full luff length for those conditions. As a result, it is not possible to tension the halyard sufficiently when the wind increases, without the sail being stretched beyond it's rated limits. This is the reason for the Cunningham, a hole placed in the luff tabling approximately between twenty to thirty centimetres up from the tack. A purchase from this hole allows the luff to be stretched tight as the wind increases without adding to the overall luff length. In moderate airs upwind, the halyard will have been tightened hard enough to draw the head of the sail up to the black band, then as the wind increases further the Cunningham can be progressively tightened. (A common fault is to over-tighten the Cunningham in an attempt to move the draft in the top of the sail. Because of the friction between the sail's luff rope and the groove in the mast, the sail will often require a quick shimmer to unstick the luff and allow the effect of the Cunningham to be transmitted to the top part of the sail. You should be aware of this when applying Cunningham.)

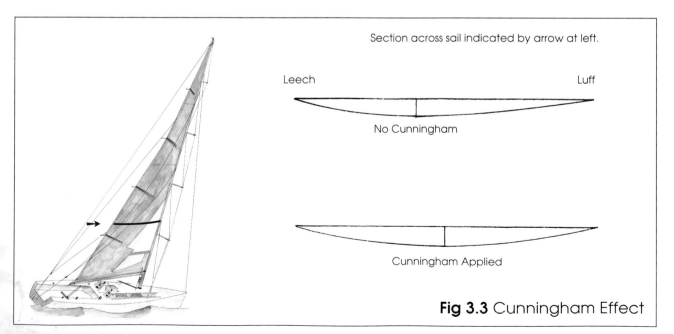

Section across sail indicated by arrow at left.

Leech   Luff

No Cunningham

Cunningham Applied

Fig 3.3 Cunningham Effect

We have already seen that forestay sag, or the lack of it, controls the actual amount of fullness in the genoa. The same basic criterion holds true for the mainsail but here the luff is controlled by the mast rather than by a flexible forestay. A mast inverted backwards in the middle is inevitably bad news; a straight mast will usually give maximum fullness in the centre of the sail. As the mast is allowed to bend forward in the middle, the luff will move away from the leech and therefore remove fullness from the sail. How mast bend is adjusted will depend on the rig, but in general, allowing the middle of the mast to bend will decrease fullness and therefore reduce power in the middle of the sail, while bending the top of the mast will do the same in the upper part of the sail.

When applied to a fractional rigged boat, this will mean that tightening the standing backstay will depower the top of the mainsail whilst increasing tension in the runners and loosening off checkstays (if fitted) will do the same for the middle of the sail. If your rig is flexible enough, it may be possible to play the standing backstay in gusty conditions to alter the power at the top of the sail as each gust hits and then dies away. Lower mast bend is normally a coarser control which will only be adjusted for the average conditions.

The amount of twist in the sail is controlled by mainsheet tension or by the kicking strap (boom vang). If you have a mainsail traveller, then it is normal to control twist when going upwind with the mainsheet. With the genoa, we saw that it was possible to look at the tell-tales on the luff to decide on the amount of twist required. With the mainsail, the luff will often be backwinded by the genoa and therefore luff tell-tales are of less importance. Here the critical area to consider is how the wind is leaving the back edge of the sail and we therefore have tell-tales placed on the leech, normally at the end of each batten pocket. If the sail is sheeted in too far, so that there is insufficient twist, the top tell-tale in particular will stall, indicating that the wind is not exiting the leech cleanly but is falling off and becoming turbulent. When this happens the sail is stalled and there is no laminar flow of air along the leeward side of the sail with the consequence that there is little drive being produced. The ideal in most conditions is to sheet the mainsail in until the top leech tell-tale is on the verge of stalling, seen by it occasionally actually stalling and disappearing behind the sail.

In very light airs the sheet should be eased so that this top tell-tale virtually never stalls, then as the wind increases to moderate, the tell-tale can be stalled for up to fifty per cent of the time. When the boat becomes overpowered and heels too much, the sail can be allowed to twist off further to spill wind from the head.

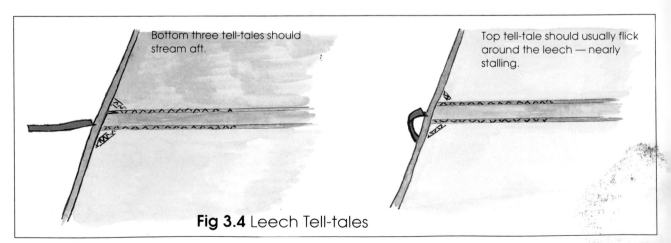

Bottom three tell-tales should stream aft.

Top tell-tale should usually flick around the leech — nearly stalling.

Fig 3.4 Leech Tell-tales

As a general principle, the tighter the leech of the mainsail, the higher the yacht will point but the slower she will go. Be careful not to overtighten the leech or it will be impossible to achieve reasonable speeds.

On a reach, the same effect can be obtained by tightening the kicking strap to control the leech tension and thus the amount of twist. The main difference when reaching is that the sail should never be allowed to stall and that slightly more twist should be allowed than is required upwind. This is because you are not trying to gain pointing height but are looking for sheer speed.

The angle of the mainsail to the wind is controlled with the traveller when going upwind and by the sheet on a reach. Taking the upwind situation first, the boom should be on or near the centreline of the boat until this starts to produce too much weather helm, then the traveller should be eased down to keep about five or six degrees of applied rudder. In gusts the traveller will need to be dropped down the track or the yacht will heel excessively, then pulled up again as the gust dies away. Never have the traveller so high that the boom is to windward of the boat's centreline as this will cause the leech of the mainsail to drive you backwards!!

If sailing in windy weather with a small, non-overlapping headsail, the traveller will probably need to be let further down the track than with an overlapping headsail because the slot between the two sails will be much wider.

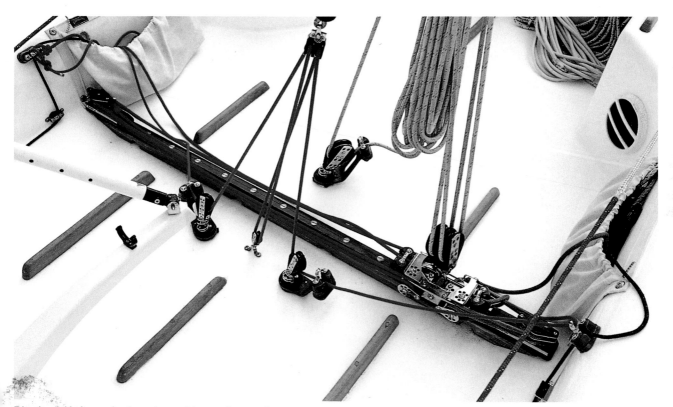

Photo 3.4 A mainsheet and traveller system at rest. Fine-sheet tune is controlled by the two swivelling blocks aft of the traveller; traveller control by the blocks at each side of the car and the primary main sheet is amidships ahead of the traveller.

Photo 3.5 The traveller is eased well down its track on this two-sail reach and the headsail has been sheeted out to the toe-rail.

On a reach, the mainsail will almost certainly need to be eased further than is possible by dropping the traveller down the track. This means that the mainsheet will not be controlling leech tension and this must therefore be done with the kicking strap. Here the leech should normally be just closed enough to keep the top tell-tale always flying and the sheet should be eased until either the luff is just about lifting or, if there are reaching tell-tales near the luff, so that these are flying correctly. In small gusts the sheet can be eased more, so that the luff is actually flapping and if still less power is needed to reduce heel, the kicking strap can also be let off to allow the sail to twist off and flap at the top.

Some boats do not have a traveller and on others the traveller is sometimes inefficient and difficult to use. In these circumstances it is possible to use the kicking strap to maintain leech tension even when going upwind, the sheet is then used to alter the angle of the sail to the wind. You will need an extremely powerful kicking strap to do this and must realise that the loads imposed on both the boom and the goose-neck will be relatively high – unless both are strong, you can cause serious damage by 'vang sheeting' in this way. If the kicking strap has been tight while going upwind, you must also remember to loosen it a bit before going off on a reach, or even bearing away to duck behind another yacht. If this is not done, the loads from the kicking strap will force the mast sideways at the goose-neck, taking the mast out of column sideways and in extreme conditions the mast might actually fracture, or if deck stepped may be forced out of the heel fitting.

Spinnakers

Spinnakers are basically large, loose-luffed sails that in most ways respond to the same controls as a genoa. If the spinnaker is set on a pole as normal, then it has the advantage that as the wind moves aft, the tack can be moved in concert with the wind and laminar airflow can thus be maintained at much greater wind angles than would be possible with a sail tacked to the boat's centreline.

Working from the front, the controls that you have over the spinnaker are:-

1. The pole position fore and aft.

This is controlled by the windward guy which should go through the end of the pole and be attached to the tack of the sail. As already stated, the pole will need to be squared back as the wind moves aft and as a general guide it should be at about right-angles to the apparent wind.

Since it is possible in light to moderate airs to reach at angles significantly less than ninety degrees and that the pole cannot be let any further forward than the forestay, it follows that the pole cannot be at right-angles to the wind when shy reaching. Therefore on a shy reach the pole will be 'over squared' by up to about twenty degrees. As the wind frees a little, the pole should be squared back so that this over squaring is gradually reduced and by the time the apparent wind is at about one hundred and five degrees to the boat, the pole is actually square to the wind.

When broad reaching or running, a more accurate guide to squaring the pole is to look at the luff of the sail. If, when sheeted so that it is just curling, the luff flies to windward of the

pole end, the pole needs to be squared aft more and conversely, if the luff is falling to leeward from the end of the pole, then the pole should be eased forward. The ideal will be when the luff of the sail is rising more or less vertically from the pole end.

2. Pole height.

The easiest way to consider correct pole height is to compare it to halyard tension on a genoa. As the pole is lowered it will stretch the luff of the sail, thus dragging some of the material from the aft part of the sail towards the front. This in turn moves the draft in the sail forward. It follows therefore, that if the wind is well forward, blowing the sailcloth back in the sail, the pole should be lower than if the wind is well aft and this is indeed the correct trim.

Because it is quite hard to see where the draft is in a spinnaker, a guide to pole height is given by the position of the luff curl as the sheet is eased. If the pole is too high the luff will curl first at the head of the sail and if the pole is too low the luff will curl first at the bottom. When the luff curls first at about the mid height of the sail, the pole height is probably about right.

3. Sheet tension.

This is the basic in and out control on the spinnaker. The sheet should nearly always be eased until the sail starts to curl along the luff. Any tighter than this and the sail will be stalled and slow, any looser and the whole sail will curl in and collapse.

Spinnaker trimming on the sheet is a job that requires immense concentration. The sheet will need to played constantly to keep the sail just on the edge of curling and any lapse in concentration always seems to lead to the whole sail collapsing.

4. Fore and aft sheet lead position.

As with a genoa, this controls the amount of twist in the leech of the sail. As the sheet is moved aft, the clew can rise allowing more twist and vice versa. In general terms, the sheet should be as far aft as possible on a close reach, gradually moving it forward as the wind squares around to a run. If the sheet is too far forward, the leech will be closed and stalled, there will be too much backwinding of the mainsail and the air in the sail will not be able to exit cleanly. Too far aft and the sail will be twisted off and the head of the sail will be spilling wind and thus losing power. Depending on the layout of the yacht, the fore and aft sheeting position may either be controlled by tweaker lines attached to the boat amidships or by judicious use of snatch-blocks on the toe-rail.

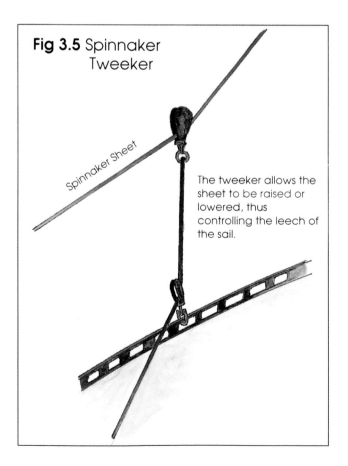

Fig 3.5 Spinnaker Tweeker

Spinnaker Sheet

The tweeker allows the sheet to be raised or lowered, thus controlling the leech of the sail.

Close Reaching with Spinnakers

Sailing on a tight reach with a spinnaker set can be exhilarating and very fast or it can be a series of panics, lurching from one broach to the next. In gusty conditions this is even more true than in steady wind. Although the helmsman is vital to the equation, the trimmer is just as important and close reaching with a really top class trimmer is a joy.

With the pole on or near the forestay, the spinnaker will be almost completely to leeward of the yacht and a large part of its power will be trying to heel the yacht and to turn her into the wind. As each gust hits, the power will immediately increase but the inertia inherent due to the weight of the yacht will prevent her from accelerating as fast. This means that in each gust, the apparent wind will not only increase but it will also move further aft and both of these factors will necessitate the sheet being eased. If the helmsman has been on the edge of control in the steady wind state, he must bear away slightly to make use of the increased power and without heeling excessively; unless the sheet is eased he will be prevented from doing so by the increased weather helm that will be experienced.

Photo 3.6→ *Corum*, a French Admiral's Cup boat, looks well under control on this fairly shy spinnaker reach. The pole is well forward but clear of the headstay – look at the sag in the headstay when the mast controls are set for off-wind sailing.

Fig 3.6 Windward Broach

1

A gust strikes the yacht on a spinnaker reach. The bow is trying to round up into the wind. The helmsman is desperately trying to bear away, but the rudder is beginning to stall and he is in danger of losing control. You should:

A Ease the mainsheet — fast.

Then if you still have control problems

B Release the kicking-strap.

C Ease the spinnaker sheet — a metre or so at a time, but try to keep the kite in the air.

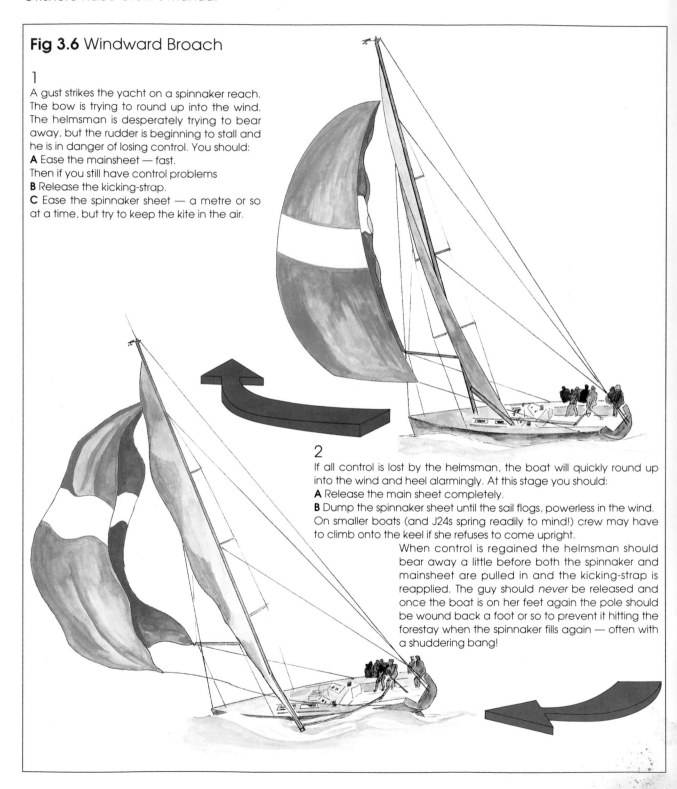

2

If all control is lost by the helmsman, the boat will quickly round up into the wind and heel alarmingly. At this stage you should:

A Release the main sheet completely.

B Dump the spinnaker sheet until the sail flogs, powerless in the wind. On smaller boats (and J24s spring readily to mind!) crew may have to climb onto the keel if she refuses to come upright.

When control is regained the helmsman should bear away a little before both the spinnaker and mainsheet are pulled in and the kicking-strap is reapplied. The guy should *never* be released and once the boat is on her feet again the pole should be wound back a foot or so to prevent it hitting the forestay when the spinnaker fills again — often with a shuddering bang!

Therefore, on a gusty reach when each gust hits, the sheet should be eased considerably and the pole will also usually need squaring a little. This will allow the extra power to be turned into acceleration forwards and will also enable the helmsman to keep the yacht under control. If the helmsman is still having trouble and has too much weather helm (tiller around his ears !) then two things must happen quickly or a broach will be the result. Power must be dumped from the back of the boat as fast as possible. The mainsheet can be let go completely which will help a little, but the leech of the mainsail will still be generating weather helm and so the kicking strap should also be dumped. At the same time the spinnaker sheet should be eased off in big armfuls, letting the luff curl more than normal but hopefully not quite allowing the whole spinnaker to collapse. As the helmsman regains full control, the spinnaker sheet can be wound in again and eventually the kicking strap can be retightened. If a broach does occur then the spinnaker sheet should be dumped completely, allowing the sail to flap. Once control has been regained and the yacht is back on course, the spinnaker will need to be over sheeted initially to get it flying again but will then need easing to its correct position.

At no time should the spinnaker guy be let forward as this will merely exacerbate the situation. Even in a wild broach with the yacht lying on its side, the guy should be kept where it was, the spinnaker will flap quite happily with the sheet let off but if the guy were to be eased as well, the sail would continue flying – but out to leeward of the boat!

Downwind Spinnaker Trim

When running as square as possible the aim should be to achieve the best possible VMG downwind. In light airs this will necessitate quite large gybing angles, with the pole quite near the forestay and the apparent wind on the beam. In stronger winds it will be possible to sail much lower and eventually in really strong winds, control will be the over riding factor in how low it is possible to sail.

Taking the light airs situation first, the trimmer will need to converse with the helmsman almost continually. If the boat speed is too low and there is little pressure in the sail, he should call for the helmsman to come up. Then as speed starts to build, the apparent wind will increase, there will be good pressure in the sail and the helmsman can sail lower again. In really steady winds it should be possible to play around with the angle for a bit and settle down to what appears to give the optimum VMG. In changing wind speeds which are normal in very light airs, the optimum angle will keep changing as well. Pressure in the sail is the guide, together with boat speed – good pressure means sail lower, little pressure forces you to sail higher.

In moderate airs, the situation is similar except that the changes in wind angle are unlikely to be quite so large. Here it is beneficial to have a set of target speeds to aim at for each wind speed so that both helmsman and trimmer have an idea of what they are trying to achieve. As with upwind sailing, the VMG meter should be used with great caution. The inertia in the yacht will prevent her from responding immediately to changes in wind speed and the average VMG needs to be looked at over a period of at least thirty seconds before changes are made to the trim and wind angle.

On a windy run the situation changes quite significantly. In this case, there will be enough pressure in the sail to run as low as you like at all times and control becomes the over riding feature. If the spinnaker is trimmed as for a moderate airs run, and eased until it curls all the time, it will cause the yacht to roll to weather in each gust. This is because, with the leech of the sail set correctly for the average wind strength, when a gust hits, the leech will stretch more and allow the head of the sail to twist off. Since the spinnaker will be eased right out because you are running, when it twists, the power from the head will be pushing the masthead to windward. At the same time as this is happening with the spinnaker, a similar thing will be happening to the mainsail. Then as the gust dies away and the leeches tighten up, the power in the top of the sails will once again be heeling the boat to leeward and a rhythmic roll has started.

In reasonable wave conditions, this sort of rolling may be acceptable and controllable, but as soon as there are any significant waves to contend with it is likely to degenerate into a battle to retain control of the boat – the death roll. The problem is that in the normal situation, with the pressure of the sails heeling the boat to leeward, the tendency will be for the boat to turn to windward. Then as a gust hits and the yacht is heeled to windward by the twisted sails, she will attempt to bear away with lee helm. This creates the danger of broaching, either to windward which is at least safe – even if slow, or to leeward which can be very dangerous because the boom may sweep across the heads of the crew and possibly slam into a runner.

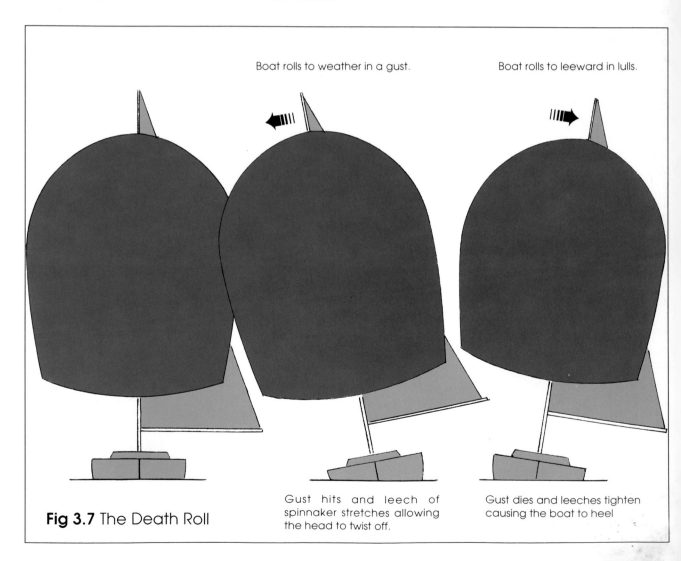

Boat rolls to weather in a gust.

Boat rolls to leeward in lulls.

Fig 3.7 The Death Roll

Gust hits and leech of spinnaker stretches allowing the head to twist off.

Gust dies and leeches tighten causing the boat to heel

There are two real options if the run is becoming uncontrolable. The first being to simply sail slightly higher on a safe broad reach. This has the obvious disadvantage that you are by definition not running square and are therefore not making the best course downwind.

The alternative is to trim the sails so that control is maintained, even at the expense of a small amount of boat speed. The mainsheet can be slightly over sheeted and the kicking strap tightened so that the mainsail is unable to twist off too much. This will tend to induce more weather helm but in itself may stop the roll to weather. So far as the spinnaker is concerned, this should be 'strapped down' to stabilise it. The pole can be lowered a bit more than normal which keeps the luff tight and the sheet should be led well forward to stop the clew rising and thus control twist. This is the steady state, marginally under control situation and at this time the sheet can be played just as normal, with the luff on edge. If there is still a tendency for the boat to roll to weather in a gust, the spinnaker sheet should be trimmed on and during the dangerous period as the gust actually hits, a slightly higher course should be sailed.

Remember that although this is a safe way to go downwind in a lot of wind, it is not so fast as having a helmsman who can control the yacht with the sails trimmed normally and if the 'strapping' of the sails is overdone, it will be slow.

If by chance you do broach to leeward and gybe inadvertently, the easiest way out is usually to gybe back again. Keep the guy where it is and let the sheet out which will allow the spinnaker to collapse. If the boom is pinned against the old runner and the mainsail is holding the boat down, get the other runner on and then let the old one go which will allow the mainsail to go right out. Then, as the boat bears away back towards her old course, trim the spinnaker sheet, get ready on the mainsheet and runners for an ordinary gybe and gybe the boat around.

The only time you might need to drop the spinnaker completely is if it has become wrapped around the forestay during the broach and will not unwrap itself.

During any broach the most important concern is safety, both for the crew and the rig. If you have not got runners there should be little danger of losing the mast and it is the heads and fingers of the crew which are at most risk. Make sure that everyone knows what to do in the event of a broach and that the critical crew (runners, mainsheet, guy and spinnaker sheet) are all well briefed. Obviously you hope that it won't happen but if you are pushing the boat hard then one day it will.

Trimming downwind in big waves is hard work but can be very rewarding. Properly trimmed, the yacht should accelerate down the face of the waves, surfing or possibly even planing like a dinghy. Badly trimmed and each wave will just be hard work for no gain.

Unless the average wind strength is very high, you will often need a combination of a gust and a wave to initiate a surf and at least one crew member should be looking behind and calling gusts and waves. As the wave approaches it will pick up the stern and will normally try to swing it around. The helmsman must be aware of this and be ready to correct early and fast rather than late and hard. As the stern comes up, the bow will point downhill and it is usually easiest for the helmsman to steer initially at least, straight down the wave. This means that as he bears away, the trimmers will need to ease out the sails but then be prepared to sheet in again as the speed picks up and the apparent wind moves forward. Then in order to maintain the surf as long as possible and to prevent the bow burying in the back of the wave ahead, the helmsman will probably need to luff along the face of the wave and the sheets will need to be trimmed in even further. Then the wave will eventually overtake you, the yacht will slow down, apparent wind will increase and move aft, the sheets will need to be eased and off we go again.

Fig 3.8 Leeward Broach

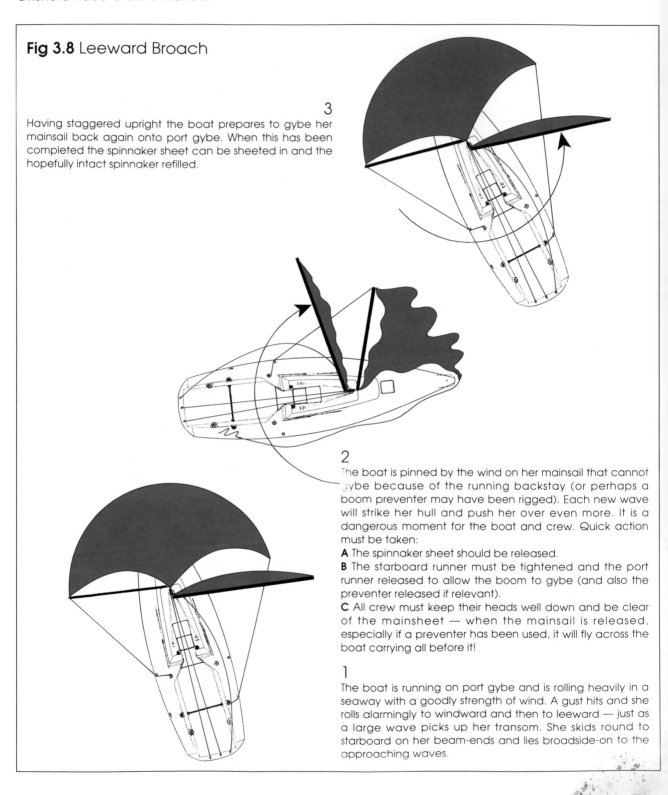

3

Having staggered upright the boat prepares to gybe her mainsail back again onto port gybe. When this has been completed the spinnaker sheet can be sheeted in and the hopefully intact spinnaker refilled.

2

The boat is pinned by the wind on her mainsail that cannot gybe because of the running backstay (or perhaps a boom preventer may have been rigged). Each new wave will strike her hull and push her over even more. It is a dangerous moment for the boat and crew. Quick action must be taken:

A The spinnaker sheet should be released.

B The starboard runner must be tightened and the port runner released to allow the boom to gybe (and also the preventer released if relevant).

C All crew must keep their heads well down and be clear of the mainsheet — when the mainsail is released, especially if a preventer has been used, it will fly across the boat carrying all before it!

1

The boat is running on port gybe and is rolling heavily in a seaway with a goodly strength of wind. A gust hits and she rolls alarmingly to windward and then to leeward — just as a large wave picks up her transom. She skids round to starboard on her beam-ends and lies broadside-on to the approaching waves.

Asymmetric Spinnakers

Asymmetric spinnakers or gennikers are halfway between a normal symmetric spinnaker and a genoa. They are set loose-luffed like any other spinnaker but can be set either from a normal spinnaker pole or from the boat's centreline on either the stem or possibly on a bowsprit.

If set from a pole, all the comments about spinnaker trim are perfectly valid. The sail will just be slightly more efficient, especially when close reaching.

Set on the centreline, whether on a bowsprit or not, the problem is that the tack cannot be moved to keep the luff of the sail facing the wind and therefore it will not be possible to sail very square – or at least not efficiently. This means that much higher gybing angles will be required in order to maintain good airflow over the sail. Set like this, the luff tension can either be adjusted by the use of a tack strop, raising the tack to reduce luff tension and allow the draft to move aft and vice versa, or by adjusting the halyard for the same purpose.

It is when you come to gybe that asymmetrics are really different and this subject has already been covered in the chapter on crew manoeuvres.
(See Fig 1.13)

Poling out a Headsail

In really heavy weather, there will come a time when even your heaviest and smallest spinnaker is too large. At this stage the best downwind sail combination will be to pole out a genoa.

The sail will usually be taken up the luff groove as normal, with the clew taken out to the end of the pole on the windward side. On most yachts it will pay to have a separate guy to control the end of the pole as well as the normal uphaul and downhaul. The sequence to set it up should go something like this:-

1. Get the pole onto the mast and attach the uphaul, downhaul and an after guy.

2. Put the bight of the lazy genoa sheet through the end of the pole while still broad reaching.

3. Top the pole and square it back using the after guy, then tension the downhaul so that the pole is solidly triangulated.

4. Sheet the sail in on the new side, easing out the leeward sheet at the same time.

5. Adjust the inboard and outboard ends of the pole so that the clew of the sail is pushed out as far as possible and so that the loads are fairly even on leech and foot.

If you are poling out a headsail on the windward side, be very careful before hoisting a second sail to leeward. With most headfoil systems, the loads are meant to be all pulling in one direction and if you put loads on both sides of the foil it is quite likely to peel it open.

In slightly less windy conditions or if you need to broad reach and cannot carry a spinnaker, it is possible to set a genoa, loose-luffed from the end of the pole just as if it were an asymmetric spinnaker.

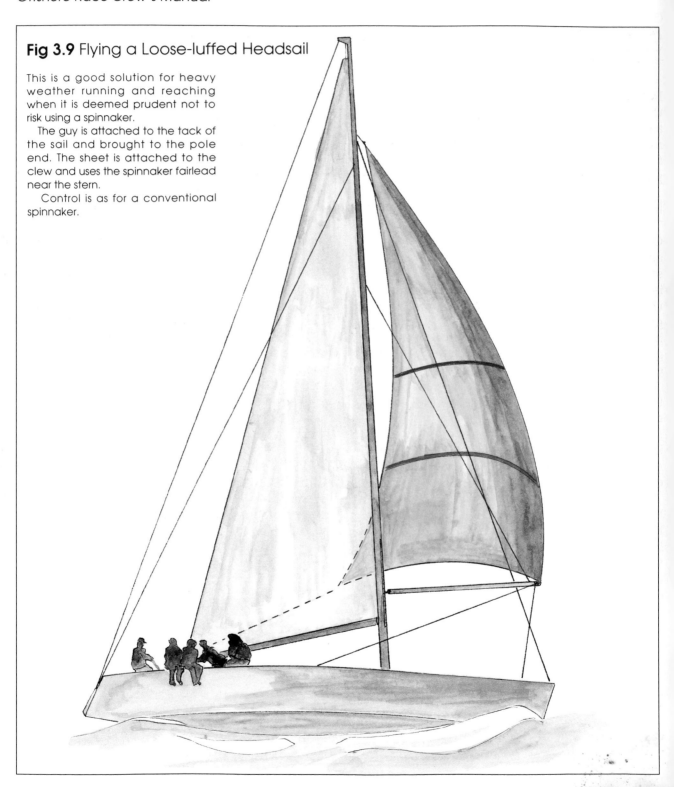

Fig 3.9 Flying a Loose-luffed Headsail

This is a good solution for heavy weather running and reaching when it is deemed prudent not to risk using a spinnaker.

The guy is attached to the tack of the sail and brought to the pole end. The sheet is attached to the clew and uses the spinnaker fairlead near the stern.

Control is as for a conventional spinnaker.

Chapter 4
Setting Up For An Offshore Race

Racing offshore needs a degree of preparation that many inshore day-racers do not appreciate. The better set up the boat and the more prepared each crew member is, then the faster you will be able to sail and the more pleasant will be the experience.

Importance of Stowage

On an inshore race, most gear will be left ashore to save weight and the problems of gear stowage do not really become apparent. Also, it is possible to sail effectively for a few hours if the area below-decks becomes a tip and generally untidy. As races get longer, it becomes ever more important to ensure that gear is stowed tidily since this will enhance efficiency and creature comforts.

I firmly believe that there should be a plan for the stowage of all gear and will look at some specific items in this short chapter. The more the interior degenerates into a mess, the harder it will be to find things when they are needed and the worse will become the living conditions for the crew.

Loose gear can present one of the greatest hazards to crew members and to the yacht in bad weather and flying cans or batteries can literally be lethal. All gear, but especially heavy items, need to be stowed in such a way that they cannot break loose whatever the boat does. Locker lids should be secure and any very heavy items should be lashed down to prevent damage.

Safety Equipment

All safety equipment must have its proper place in the stowage plan and the entire crew should know where the different items are to be found so that no time is lost in an emergency. Where gear is stowed in lockers, it is a good idea to label the outside of the lockers to indicate their content.

If life-jackets or safety harnesses need to be adjusted before being worn these should be labelled individually and adjusted for each crew member before the race starts. Wasting time and effort down below in adjusting this sort of equipment during a race is a sure way to put people off wearing it. There are two different bodies of opinion on the stowage of such items. One says that they should be kept with personal gear so that each individual knows where to find his own. My attitude is that, once correctly adjusted, the harnesses and life-jackets should be re-stowed centrally; this is for two reasons. In an emergency they can be grabbed quickly for donning as necessary and secondly one crew member can be sent below to get equipment for all the crew, without the need to rummage through a number of bags.

Other gear such as tool boxes, bolt/wire cutters, radar reflector and so on should all have their places. Equipment that may not be obvious in its operation will need to have instructions along with it. This includes the first-aid kit, which under most racing regulations requires a manual to be included. Assuming that your kit has at least some drugs included for offshore races, it is vital that full instructions on their use is kept with the kit – normal chemists notes such as 'take one tablet three times a day' are really not sufficient.

It can be worth splitting the first-aid kit into two or possibly three parts. One small 'ready use' kit with plasters for minor cuts and small rope burns, seasick pills, headache pills and not much else. The rest of the first-aid kit can usefully be split into a bandages and dressings box plus a separate pills, creams and ointments box. All should have a list of contents which is checked on a regular basis to ensure the contents are kept replenished and in good condition.

The liferaft is one of the most important items of safety equipment and will need careful consideration as to where it is stowed. It is by nature a heavy parcel that should be positioned well away from the bow and stern of the boat and preferably somewhere low down so that it will assist stability. Current Offshore Racing Council special regulations allow the raft to be stowed in one of three following ways

a) In a cockpit locker – if that locker is solely there for the raft.
b) On deck.
c) Below deck.

If stowed below, which is considered the best place in the majority of cases, the raft must weigh less than 40kgs and should be located – 'adjacent to the main companionway'. In practice this means that most rafts of up to eight-man capacity can be stowed in this manner. They should be kept on the cabin sole and in a position where they can be readily accessed. The regulations also state that the crew must be capable of getting the raft(s) to the side-deck within fifteen seconds. This latter rule should encourage stowage in a position where they are unlikely to become buried under sails and also the adoption of a method of secure fastening that can be released quickly.

Torches and Batteries

The torches carried aboard are of different design and used for a variety of purposes. In fact they come under the headings of safety, deck equipment and personal equipment depending on their use.

When racing overnight, every crew member needs a small personal torch. These can range from cheap disposable items that are unlikely to survive more than one wet and windy race, to nicely made, fully waterproof and shockproof torches. So long as they work when needed it does not matter much. From an owner's point of view, this is one item of gear which tends to 'walk' as the crew leave after a race. Personal torches should be stowed with individual gear and not stuffed into the chart table. I normally keep mine in my oilskin jacket pocket on the basis that I will be wearing that during most night watches.

Deck torches for illumination of sails, other competitors, halyards at the masthead and so on, need to be powerful and ideally should be operable with one hand and have a beam that can be focused. These boat torches should be stowed in a central position so that any crew member can quickly find one when needed. It is worthwhile investing in one or more adjustable clamps to hold a torch in a set position; it can then be used to illuminate the genoa tell-tales, (Important on a dark night when both the helmsman and trimmers need see the tell-tales to maintain optimum performance) – otherwise one crew member will get pretty bored pointing a torch for the whole watch. These clamps should obviously be stowed with the torches themselves.

Spare batteries and bulbs should be carried and must be kept dry. Batteries in particular are heavy and their stowage should be relatively low in the yacht; they also need to be secured against the possibility of knockdowns or other unwanted gyrations.

Personal Gear

There are two main considerations with personal gear for offshore racing. The first of these is the decision of what to take and the second is how and where to stow the necessary items.

Personal kit should be kept to a sensible minimum, but there are seldom circumstances when I would go to sea for more than an a few hours without a set of waterproofs. There

Torches have been set up to shine on a pair of headsail luff tell-tales and a mainsail leech tell-tale.

The white light at the masthead is the aft sector of the tricolour navigation light. It will probably also illuminate the Windex.

The only other lights are dulled (usually red) and are the steering compasses and instrument repeaters.

Light from the interior should be kept to a minimum.

Fig 4.1
Night Racing

maybe the odd occasion when oilskins are not needed, but there are not too many places where night sailing is comfortable without some form of protective wind and waterproof clothing. The weight of oilskins can be modified according to the time of year and where you are sailing. What is suitable for a beat in the English Channel in early spring may be positively uncomfortable and hot if used in the Mediterranean in high summer. I have three types of oilskins and wear each according to the prevailing conditions. This may seem extravagant, but each set lasts much longer than they otherwise would – having said that, I probably sail more days per year than most people and this helps to make it worthwhile having the right clothes for a variety of conditions.

I have a set of heavyweight, foul weather offshore oilskins. Most leading brands provide built-in personal safety with this type and I would suggest that as a minimum they should include a life-harness, life-jacket, whistle and reflective patches. Other potential life-savers that can be carried include personal EPIRBs, light-sticks and homing devices, but in fact advances in this area are so fast that any complete list of recommendations would be obsolete before this book hits the press. I also have a slightly lighter set of full oilskins for summer wear, especially for nasty weather when day sailing – lighter and more flexible, they do not provide the warmth and protection of my foul weather suit but are more comfortable for round-the-cans racing. At the light end of the scale, I have a lightweight smock together with breathable trousers which makes the ideal combination for sailing in hot weather, when all that is really required is a spray suit.

Photo 4.1 A good pair of heavy weather offshore oilskins *(Courtesy of Henri Lloyd)*

Photo 4.2 Medium weight waterproofs for warmer conditions *(Courtesy of Henri Lloyd)*

Apart from oilskins, other clothing for yacht racing needs to be light and if it needs to be warm, it should stay warm even when wet. The modern insulating materials such as 'Thinsulate' provide this type of warmth and are incredibly light when compared to traditional woollen garments. I have a two-piece thermal underwear suit; a mid-layer spray-proof insulated jacket and salopettes and thermal pullovers. These combined with double-loop knitted ski socks and a warm hat make up my total cold weather clothing.

In warm weather, shorts and a polo shirt are often all that is required during the day, but unless the nights are incredibly warm, I would not like to do an offshore race without at least the mid-layer clothes being available.

So far as footwear is concerned, a choice between sailing boots and shoes is a pleasant luxury. Many yacht skippers, where weight is